FROM
LISHAMIE

THEYTUS BOOKS

Library and Archives Canada Cataloguing in Publication

Canadien, Albert, 1945-
From Lishamie / by Albert Canadien.

Includes bibliographical references.
ISBN 978-1-894778-65-7

1. Canadien, Albert, 1945-. 2. Tinne Indians--Social life and customs.
3. Tinne Indians--Residential schools. 4. Tinne Indians--Biography.
I. Title.

E99.T56C35 2010   971.9'30049720092   C2010-901343-3

Printed in Canada by Gauvin Press

RECYCLED
Paper made from
recycled material
FSC® C100212

Printed on Ancient Forest Friendly 100% post consumer fibre paper.

THEYTUS BOOKS

www.theytus.com
In Canada: Theytus Books, Green Mountain Rd., Lot 45, RR#2, Site 50, Comp. 8
Penticton, BC, V2A 6J7, Tel: 250-493-7181
In the USA: Theytus Books, P.O. Box 2890, Oroville, Washington, 98844

  Patrimoine   Canadian
canadien   Heritage

 Canada Council Conseil des Arts
for the Arts   du Canada

 BRITISH COLUMBIA
ARTS COUNCIL

Theytus Books acknowledges the support of the following:
We acknowledge the financial support of the Government of Canada
through the Book Publishing Industry Development Program (BPIDP)
for our publishing activities. We acknowledge the support of the Canada
Council for the Arts which last year invested $20.1 million in writing and
publishing throughout Canada. Nous remercions de son soutien le Conseil
des Arts du Canada, qui a investi 20,1 millions de dollars l'an dernier dans
les lettres et l'édition à travers le Canada. We acknowledge the support
of the Province of British Columbia through the British Columbia Arts
Council.

From Lishamie

Albert Canadien

*I'd like to dedicate this book to
my wife, Kawennakatste (aka Esther);
my children: Rory-Jon, Tara and Tasha;
all of my grandchildren;
my brother Archie
and the people of Lishamie.*

PROLOGUE

In this memoir, I've tried to convey how we, the Dene children, used to live on the land with our parents before we were put into residential schools. Our lives were completely different from the Indian children down south on reservations. We did not have reservations in the Northwest Territories; we lived on the land and moved to traditional hunting and fishing areas. We were not confined within an area. We had mobility, which was essential for our traditional way of life. We did not think it was a hardship to paddle fifty miles to a fishing area or travel by dog team for a day or two to reach our trapping area. This was our way of life. This was the kind of life I was born into and experienced before being put into residential school.

We, the Dene people, were one of the last First Nations to be affected by western society. Most of our people lived in the interior of the Northwest Territories, where contact was minimal or non-existent. Since the first European contact in Canada in the early 1500s, our people, in what is now the Deh Cho region, saw very little of the white people. It was only later that our ancestors saw the first white man, in 1789, when Alexander Mackenzie travelled down the Deh Cho, which was later named after him as the Mackenzie River. Thereafter, the fur trade brought in more white people.

According to information from the Dene Nation Office in Yellowknife, there were 137 non-Dene people in the Mackenzie District in 1901; that number went up to 519 in 1911, and they just kept coming.

Late contact had its advantages because we have been able to carry on with our culture and traditions of on-land activities to this day. Granted, there were some prohibitions on certain traditional ceremonies by the early missionaries and government. The missionaries probably regarded some of these ceremonies as sinful acts, and some were likely punishable by law.

The Dene culture is an oral culture, as opposed to the written culture of western society. In an oral culture, language is essential to transmit knowledge; therefore, language is an integral part of that culture. It carries detailed traditional knowledge of the land, environment, plants, fish and animals. This knowledge includes beliefs, customs, values, history, and the achievements of the Dene people, and it has been handed down through stories from generation to generation.

Our people pursued a subsistence way of life, and today, in most Dene communities, this is still being done, although on a smaller scale.

The subsistence way of life was far different from the sedentary agricultural lifestyle of western society. It was a way of life that depended on an individual's skills and knowledge of seasonal changes, an essential part of living off the land. It was the ability to recognize certain plants for their medicinal value; the ability to learn and understand the movements and habits of animals, and so on. It was a simple way of life, with respect for land and nature. There was no accumulation of non-essential material. Maybe that's why some early European explorers thought the Indian culture was a poor one; they did not see piles of surplus material they were accustomed to.

The subsistence way of life involved taking what one needed now and making use of it wisely to survive. It was a simple means of conservation, by not depleting the animals you depended on for your livelihood. The Dene way of life was not based on competition, hoarding and self-interest. The traditional habit of sharing had meaning; people looked after each other and conformed to traditions and customs.

Dene spirituality is not a religion as is commonly defined today. Religion is generally based upon written doctrine and instruction, such as the catechism. Dene spirituality is based on stories that were handed down to explain creation, visions, animals and some natural forces. Over time, these stories have become a fixed belief in the traditions and cultures of our people.

The Dene had been on this land pursuing traditional activities and living in permanent traditional villages long before the missionaries arrived and established schools and churches. The arrival of the Catholic missionaries had a great impact on the traditional lifestyle of our people, especially on our traditional beliefs. In Fort Providence, the Grey Nuns of Montreal arrived in 1867 and established the first residential school.

After living traditionally on the land with my family, being at the residential school was an abrupt change for me. My life at the residential school was structured around a rigid lifestyle, right down to going to sleep, waking up, going to church, learning, working and eating. A clock, and someone else's rules, now governed my life. I was forbidden to speak my own language and was given religious instructions, not necessarily on how to be a good human being, but rather on how to be a good Catholic. Fortunately, I was able to go home for two months every summer until I eventually moved away from my community.

During my summers at home, we continued our traditional activities on the land and we continued to speak in our own language. We moved to a certain area when the fishing was plentiful. We lived in tents with spruce boughs covering the floor. After a couple of weeks, we'd move to another area and back to Lishamie, our traditional village, for berry picking. Sometimes I went with my dad or brothers on hunting trips for big game or ducks. We made offerings to the water before setting out on the river or lake on a hunting trip. I learned through hands-on experience or by watching and re-membering. As children, we did not have toys to play with, but we played games based on traditional activities, such as hunting, fishing, and storytelling. Then, by the beginning of September, our parents reluctantly brought us back to the residential school for another year.

I experienced physical abuse in the residential school at the hands of my religious supervisors. When that happened, sometimes I would cry, but other times I wouldn't. It seemed the more you cried, the more you were punished, so I learned ways to hide my emotions. I was fortunate that I did not experience sexual abuse, but there were other forms of abuse, including mental and emotional abuse.

Writing about my life has been my way of dealing with the residential school experience. Initially, I just wrote down all I could remember, without any emotion, until I finally completed the draft of my story. Then one day, I read my story and the experience of re-remembering it affected me emotionally. At times, I had tears in my eyes and I couldn't read any further. I mentioned this to my wife, who is a healing counsellor, and she explained that I was detached from my feelings as I wrote, but now as I read certain sections, I was reliving the experience, reconnecting with the thoughts and feelings of that time.

Today, I feel I'm in the transition stage on my own personal healing journey. To a certain extent, I think I've come to terms with what happened to me at the residential school. But I still struggle sometimes when I remember certain things from those years. I don't think my situation is unique. I think most of us Dene people are in various stages of transition, still trying to cope with all that happened to us not only at the residential school, but since first contact.

For a very long time I had difficulty with forgiveness. I even shied away from thinking about it. I believed that forgiveness was to pardon someone, to start with a new, clean page as though nothing had happened. Forgiveness may be healing, but one cannot ignore the wrong that was done. Now at this stage of my life, I think I can forgive, but there are some things I will never forget.

Albert J. Canadien
Yellowknife, NT
May 2007

Fort Providence, NWT

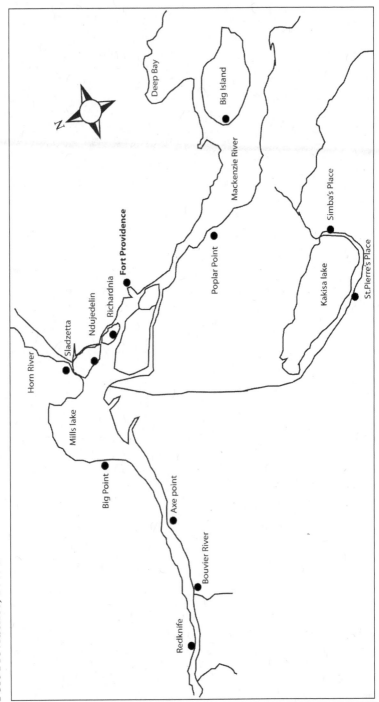

Map used by permission of the Fort Providence Hamlet Council 2007

CHAPTER ONE

Late one Friday evening, I was driving out of Yellowknife, heading to the highway that would take me to my hometown of Fort Providence for a weekend hunting trip. I turned the radio on to keep me company until the signal faded away. I would be able to pick up the signal as I went by Fort Rae and again when I got to Fort Providence. I planned to stay at my cabin, which was nestled on the shore of the Mackenzie River not too far from town. I was hoping for a chance to go to Lishamie, my traditional village, where I grew up. As I rolled along, I thought of collecting some firewood and maybe shooting a couple of ducks on my way there. The ducks would make a tasty dinner.

My thoughts were suddenly interrupted by what I heard over the radio. The announcer had said something about The Chieftones. I reached over and turned up the volume. Sure enough, it was The Chieftones and I was singing *Running Bear*. I hadn't heard that song for ages and I listened until it was over.

The song led my thoughts back to an earlier time, to a small recording studio someplace outside of Chicago — was the town called Lake Geneva. It was so long ago. And it was a long, some might say improbable, journey from my boyhood days in Lishamie all the way to playing onstage with a band at Madison Square Gardens and Boston Gardens, and to being opening acts for bands like the Beach Boys and Jerry Lee Lewis.

As the song faded into another, my thoughts came back to the present as I continued down the highway, finally arriving at my cabin in the early morning hours. I slept for a few hours and then drove to the gas station to fill up my vehicle and get coffee. There I met my cousin, Louis, who was filling up some jerry cans. He was going to the Mills Lake area to hunt and asked if I wanted to come along. I didn't hesitate; I was ready to go.

On the way down the Mackenzie River, I asked if we could go through the channel that flowed by Lishamie. The water was high this time of the year so the channel was not too shallow. We stopped the kicker and drifted slowly with the current. Back then, everyone referred to any outboard motor as a kicker, just as they do today. I closed my eyes and tried to remember Lishamie as it used to be. A smiling boy was playing by the shore; smoke from a big log house swirled up from the trees; the voices of my happy family speaking our language — South Slavey.

As we drifted closer, I opened my eyes to see how different a place my old traditional village had become. It was now overgrown with willows and aspen; only a couple of houses remained. The log house that belonged to Jean Marie — the old headman from our village — was still standing, although the roof had long ago caved in from heavy snow. Uncle Harry's log house had collapsed, leaving only the walls standing. The only other remains of my once-thriving village were the foundation outlines of the other log houses, which were all gone.

Memories of my childhood flooded my mind as we slowly drifted by Lishamie. I remember running down the trail to Grandfather's house, laughing and playing with the other kids along the shore. With mixed emotions, I watched the remnants of the two log houses slowly go out of sight. I thought, one day I would come back and build a cabin there just to keep in touch with a place that had been and still remains such a great part of my childhood. After all, life really began for me at Lishamie.

FROM LISHAMIE

CHAPTER 2

Lishamie was our permanent traditional village located on a large island on the north side of the Mackenzie River. There were five log houses situated on the banks of a small channel which flowed around the island and eventually back into the Mackenzie River some five miles or so downstream and about a mile from *Tuah*, or Mills Lake.

The first log house you'd see when you came downstream belonged to Jean Marie. As our village headman, he was like a spokesperson and usually sat with the chief during treaty meetings. The next house belonged to my Uncle Harry, my mother's older brother. Then there was my dad's log house; the next house belonged to Uncle Pierre and the last log house belonged to Grandfather.

There is a story about how our village got its name; how true it is I don't know, but the story goes that years ago there lived an old French trapper in the area. His name was Richard (pronounced Ree-shard). He had fishnets set up at the mouth of the small channel.

Eventually, the local people referred to the area as "Lishamie." The literal translation from the South Slavey language means "Richard's fishnets". However, in proper English, it would be "the place where Richard sets his fishnets". *Lisha* stands for the rough South Slavey pronunciation of the French name Richard

(Ree-shard), and *mih* is the South Slavey word for fishnets. So the story goes, that's how our little village derived its name and since then it has always been referred to as Lishamie.

During the winter months, we stayed in Lishamie while my dad and other men from our village went trapping. In the summer, we moved about to other places where the fish and game were plentiful. This was a time when the Dene people still lived off the land and stayed at various permanent traditional camps and villages, each with its own South Slavey name. There were other places where people gathered during the spring, summer and fall.

This was the kind of life I was born into and the only kind of life I knew while growing up. I was told that I was born on an island on the Mackenzie River, close to the settlement of Fort Providence. With no highway running by the settlement, there were very few outside influences. It was great growing up in this kind of traditional environment. I had freedom, to a certain extent, to do what I wanted. There was no clock to tell me it was time for this and time for that. I played with other kids. We didn't have toys but we played traditional games. My childhood was filled with carefree days. Best of all, there was time spent with my parents. They were always close by when I needed them. Little did I know that this carefree living would one day come to an end and change my life.

Early in the fall before the leaves fell, the men built something like a breakwater along the shore. These were twelve to fifteen feet or more in length. They were built with dried poles hammered into the river bottom with axes or homemade wooden mallets. Lengths of aspen, and willows complete with branches and leaves, were placed length-wise between these poles. The branches were then pushed down into the water between the poles, and more branches placed on top.

Once completed, this miniature dam slowed down the river and created a large eddy, which stirred up the water and, in turn, attracted the whitefish, which ran upstream in the fall. A net was tied to one of the poles and stretched downstream into the eddy. The net was checked morning and evening, and sometimes in the afternoon.

The whitefish were unloaded off the canoe back in camp, which was on the south side of the island. Some fish were cleaned and prepared for eating right away and some were fixed to dry. The remaining whitefish were left whole, and a narrow slit was made below the tail fin with a knife. A length of stick was then passed through the slits, skewering eight to ten fish in place. The fish were then hung between two poles, sometimes three or four high, in a covered log shed. The hung fish served as food for the families and their dogs in the wintertime. Dog teams were the only means of transportation in the winter, so the owners made sure they were fed and always took good care of them.

I often went with my dad and brothers when they hauled the fish by canoe back to our village. We'd paddle upriver and return down the channel with the current to our village. Once we landed, the men would haul the fish up the steep riverbank and hang them in the shed behind the house. The return trip was similar, up the channel against the current and down with the current to our fishing camp.

As the weather grew colder and the first snow came to stay, we used a dog team to haul the fish on the overland trail back to our village for storage. The fishing continued until the snow completely covered the ground and ice formed along the shore, making it difficult and dangerous to launch and land the canvas-covered canoes.

One day, shortly after we had returned to our village from the fishing camp, it began to snow again. For us, snow was fun. Just like kids in other communities in the north, this meant: "dog-team!" Nowadays, it's "Ski-Doos!"

My brother, Archie, hitched up two dogs to a small toboggan. My other brother, Daniel, put a blanket in the toboggan. I was standing by watching when, suddenly, one of them picked me up and put me in the toboggan. I didn't say anything; I didn't have time to say anything. I was placed in the blanket and they secured me inside so I wouldn't fall out. Archie yelled at the dogs and away I went by myself down the trail and among the houses. My brothers stood back and laughed at what to them must have been a funny sight.

While this was going on, my mother was busy in the house. She was sometimes a little over-protective of me as I was the only child home at the time. I remember her as being a loving and gentle mother. She would show me how to do things in detail, unlike my dad, who did things and told me to watch. My mother showed me how to tie a knot to make a loop on a rabbit snare and what kind of stick to use to hold the snare in place over the rabbit trail. She even showed me how to make sinew thread for sewing moccasins. She was stern at times, but I don't remember her ever striking my sister or me in anger. When I did something and she was close by, I would look at her for a reaction. If she smiled, then I knew she was okay with what I was doing.

Now, here I was in a small toboggan with a runaway dog team. I was really scared and started yelling, "Whoa! Whoa!"

as the little toboggan swung from side to side. The dogs didn't listen to me; they just kept on running. I was scared that I might tip over, or worse yet, that I would meet another dog team. Finally, to my relief, the team stopped when a part of the harness got snagged on the corner of one of the houses and overturned. It was funny for my brothers but it sure wasn't funny for me. One of them ran up to me, pulled the toboggan upright and loosened the harness. He quickly wiped the snow off my face with his warm hands. Then the dog team pulled the toboggan, with me still strapped in it, back to our house. One of my brothers was taking me out of the toboggan when my mother came out of the house and asked what all the commotion was about. She was totally unaware of what had happened and my brothers weren't about to tell. I didn't say anything, either.

Although I call them my brothers, Archie and Daniel are not my biological brothers. Their parents passed away when they were very young, and they grew up with their grandparents and with my mom and dad. Daniel was the younger of the two and stayed with us most of the time. Archie stayed with the grandparents and did what he could to help them around the house. He eventually got married and moved to his in-laws' camp at Big Point. I grew up thinking that they were my brothers; no one said anything different. It was much later on that I found out how they came to be with my family. But that made no difference to me; they were and are still my brothers. To this day, I still call them my brothers and their children call me their uncle. As I grew up, their grandparents became my grandparents. As a matter of fact, all the children in our village called them Grandfather and Grandmother. We were a close-knit family in a close-knit family-oriented village.

Sometime after that first snowfall, the men began to get ready for the coming trapping season. Preparation included making bait, cleaning traps, making snares, and repairing snowshoes, harnesses and sleds. There was also the hauling and stock-piling of firewood for the women who would remain behind in the village. The women also helped with preparations by making dried fish and bannock, which were placed in the porches or outside sheds to freeze.

During the summer, my dad had made a pair of snowshoe frames out of birch or spruce, held together with sinew and babiche. Babiche was a long, thin, narrow strip cut from a piece of rawhide. These strips were usually soaked in water before using, which made them much easier to work with and to thread through holes in the wooden frame. There were carved-out holes and notches on the frame where wooden pieces were fitted into place and held there with sinew or narrow strips of babiche. The frames had been hung in the house during the summer to dry into shape properly. They were now ready for the babiche webbing. My dad spread a large piece of canvas on the floor and placed the snowshoe frames, a bundle of sinew thread, and some babiche on it. Then he started to work on the snowshoes.

I remember my dad spoke French fluently and he also spoke English. He spoke in these languages when he had to, especially when he had to go to the store or to the mission. He and my mother and the other members of our village always spoke to me in our language—South Slavey.

My dad was a practical man and did things out of necessity, things that needed to get done to live off the land. He did not elaborate on the purpose of whatever he was doing, but he always told me to watch and remember. He did show me how to skin a rabbit and prepare it for cooking, and how to pluck a duck and singe it before cutting it up. There was a certain way to cut up a duck, which leaves it in one whole piece. It took me a long time before I was able to do this perfectly, and I still use that skill to this day. My relationship with my dad was just something natural. He had the experience and skills, and I needed to learn from him while growing up. I think my dad took the responsibility of looking after his family quite seriously.

I sat on the floor and watched my dad as he interlaced the long strips of babiche this way and that way, over, under and across. When the webbing was done on one snowshoe frame, he hung it on the wall by the woodstove so the babiche would dry. Then he worked on the other frame. It took a while before all the webbing was complete. Next, my dad made straps out of tanned moose hide. One strap was tied to the middle wooden piece of the snowshoe frame. He did the same with the other strap. Then he tried the straps over the heel and toe of his moccasins. He made some adjustments and without using his hands, put the snowshoe straps on with just a few motions of the foot. Then he took them off, again with just a few motions of the foot. The snowshoes were now complete and ready for use.

The men left for their traplines when there was enough snow on the ground and the ice was thick enough and safe to travel on. Some of them would travel up the Horn Plateau to Mink Lake, and still others went to areas across the Mackenzie River. There was no defined territory, as such, for any individual. The men simply went to their usual trapping areas.

The Dene of Fort Providence *(Zhahti Kue)* had their customary hunting and trapping ranges. These extended to the Deep Bay area; up the northern shore of the Great Slave Lake; the mouth of the Mackenzie River area; to the Horn Plateau; to Redknife River and areas of the southern part of the Mackenzie River. Some traplines did cross each other, but it did not create any conflict. There was an understood principle among the Dene people that no one had the right to prevent others from getting food and shelter from the land. This is based on our people's age-old traditional knowledge and understanding of the difficult conditions of the land and a value system developed from that understanding. Informally, the young people at that time all learned this value system from an early age by watching and listening to our parents and elders. Unfortunately, there is very little evidence of this being carried on today.

Some of the trappers from our village returned once or twice to get more store-bought supplies and go right back out on the trap line. Some others won't come back until a few days before Christmas or New Year. When the men were away on long hunting trips, or were gone for a long time trapping, the women usually got together. They would gather at someone's house to sew new moose hide slippers and mukluks or repair old ones, or to help another woman repair a tent or toboggan cover. Sometimes they got together just to play cards to pass the time away. I remember the women in our village played games of checkers. At that time, I didn't know the game was called checkers. To me it was just a game women played.

The homemade checker board was drawn on a large piece of cardboard. The round checker pieces were cut and made out of willows or aspen. The face of one set was marked and the other set was left plain. The women took turns playing this game while we stood or knelt around them, watching curiously. I, for one, did not understand the purpose of the game. While they played, one woman would say something like, "I'm going to steal from you," then laugh as she took a checker piece from the other player. There was always laughter at such gatherings. No one spoke English; everyone spoke South Slavey.

Sometimes, Grandmother or another woman would tell stories. I remember she was a small woman, slightly bent with age, yet she carried herself with dignity. I never knew her English name; we all called her *Etsuh,* which simply means "Grandmother" in South Slavey. She was a woman who knew a lot about the Dene way of life. Her stories were about our people and about individual men or women from long ago. Some were about a great hunter, or about someone who performed special deeds with his or her medicine. These were stories that she had heard at a very young age.

Grandmother would sit on a folded blanket on the floor while we sat close to her, next to the warm woodstove. Usually she had a cup of tea beside her and would light a small pipe before beginning her story telling. As she spoke, she would place her pipe next to her cup of tea. Sometimes she would pick up her pipe and use it to demonstrate a certain action in the story.

One evening, she told us a story about a young woman who lived with her new husband in a large teepee by a creek. There was lots of firewood close by, and large spruce trees that provided shelter from the winter winds.

One day, while her husband was away hunting for moose, a young man arrived at her camp. As he approached the teepee, she recognized him as her cousin, her uncle's youngest son. He was also hunting for moose or caribou. She fed him some rabbit meat and they talked for a long time, mostly about her parents. She wanted to know how they were doing and where they were camping for the winter. The next morning, after eating some more rabbit meat, the young man got ready to leave. Just then, they heard the noise of her husband returning from the moose hunt.

He saw the young man and glanced angrily at his young wife, asking, "Is this the way you're going to be when I go hunting?" But before she could answer, he pushed her away and roughly grabbed the young man and pushed him head first out of the teepee. The young man hurriedly got up and ran off into the bushes.

The husband began packing all their belongings into a large bag. Then he told her to take off her clothes. She began to cry, as slowly and reluctantly she removed them. Suddenly, he tore the clothes off her and she sat naked on the spruce bough floor. She tried to explain that the young man was her cousin but the husband wasn't listening. He stomped angrily on the fire to make sure there were no coals left burning. Then he left without another word.

The young woman sat on the spruce bough floor with her arms around her shoulders and sobbed. Through her tears, she looked at the pile of ashes in the fireplace. She picked up a short stick and began to poke into the ashes, all the while saying to the fire, "Grandfather, your grandchild is freezing, please light up."

Then to her surprise, she found a small glowing coal. She picked up other pieces of burned-out coal and placed them around the glowing coal. Then gently, she blew on the small pile until all the coals began to glow red. Collecting some dried moss from the inside wall of the teepee, she placed this on the glowing coals. Soon, she had a small fire burning.

Then she remembered there was a dried spruce log with long branches close to the teepee. Naked, she ran out, quickly broke off a few dried branches and ran back into the teepee. She did this several times until finally she had a pile of branches and sticks for firewood. The teepee slowly warmed up and she looked around for something she could use. All she found were a pair of rabbit feet. Carefully, she pulled short strands of sinew off the two feet and made a length of thread.

Then with a short stick, she dug into the floor of the teepee and pulled out a length of root. She pounded the root until it was almost in shreds. Then she put the length of shredded root and rabbit sinew thread in her hands, rolling the two together over her knee until she had a length just long enough to make a rabbit snare.

When she was done, she went out and walked on top of the log by the teepee. At the end of the log was a stand of small spruce trees with many rabbit trails there. She quickly set the snare and ran back to the teepee. Later that evening, she heard the cry of a rabbit. Quickly, she ran out and returned with it. Now she had fresh rabbit meat and more sinew to make another snare. When she had two rabbits, she turned the skins inside out and pulled them over her feet. Her feet were now covered and warm. She went out and set more snares and caught more rabbits.

Soon, she had enough rabbit skins to make herself an outfit. With the sharp point of a broken rabbit leg bone, she cut the skins into strips and began to weave the strips together. She made herself a pair of rabbit skin pants, then a coat. She also made herself a pair of rabbit skin shoes, which she pulled over the ones she already had on her feet. Now she was ready to go anywhere.

She wanted to find her parents, so that evening she got ready for her journey. She made a length of string from the rabbit snares, which she could unravel if she had to set more snares. Then later, she cooked as much rabbit meat as she could carry.

Early the next morning, she walked into the bush to begin her journey. She walked for many days and nights, and her supply of rabbit meat was running low. Then one morning, she came upon a small lake. In the distance, she saw smoke from a camp. She walked in the direction of the smoke and found her parents' camp. That's how the young girl came back to her parents.

Grandmother told us in our language, "It was very hard for the young girl, but she tried her best and overcame a difficult situation. She was a smart girl because she listened to her parents and now she knew what to do to survive in the bush. This is why it is important to listen and learn from your parents and the elders."

The story finished, Grandmother picked up her small pipe and reached over for the candle. With the flame of the candle she lit her pipe and enjoyed the last mouthful of tea from her cup. When we asked to hear more stories, Grandmother would tell us to bring in another load of firewood. We'd run outside, and if there was no firewood already cut, we'd saw some up and bring it in. Grandmother was a smart woman. It was one way of having firewood cut and brought into her house.

Sometimes when we were bringing in the wood, the northern lights would come out into the night sky. We watched as they danced above us, showing off their different colours.

Someone said that if you rubbed your fingernails together, the northern lights would come down. So we'd walk down the trail away from the house, rub our fingernails together for a few seconds and run like hell back to the house. Then we'd look out the window to see if the northern lights had really come down.

Another person said that if one whistled out loud, the northern lights would come down. So again, we'd walk down the trail, stand still and whistle out loud, and then run like hell again back to the house. We'd look out the window again, but the northern lights were still shining way up in the night sky. We'd laugh when one of the kids couldn't whistle but just blew out air between his lips. Although we'd continue to run down the trail and whistle a number of times, to our disappointment, the northern lights never did come down.

One of the women told us that the northern lights were like spirits from the moon. When the moon wasn't shining, these spirits, in the form of light, would come out of the moon and brighten up the night. These were good spirits because their lights helped hunters and trappers find their way back to their camps at night. In the spring, the northern lights all travel to the other side of the world and come back the following winter. It's like the thunder that travels south in the fall and returns in the spring with the birds.

Sometimes when we got too noisy, one of the women would tell us stories to keep us quiet. I remember another story that Grandmother told us: this one was also about a young woman who was newly wed to a great hunter.

One day, the young woman said they were almost out of meat, so the husband left on a hunting trip for several days, tracking a moose in the deep snow until he finally killed it.

This one moose would provide them with enough meat to last them for a long time. He skinned the moose and shaped the hide into a sled, with the fur on the outside, and left it to freeze overnight. The next day, he put as much moose meat into the makeshift sled as it could hold and began his journey home.

On the evening of the third day, he finally saw the fire light from his teepee. As he approached, he heard laughter and stopped to listen. The laughter was a blend of male and female voices. He left the moose hide sled and walked quietly towards the teepee. He peeked in and saw his wife with another man. They were holding each other, talking, giggling and laughing out loud. He stood up and his heart began to fill with anger. This must have been the reason why she sent him away on a hunting trip, he thought to himself.

He picked up his bow and arrows and quietly walked around the teepee. He found a small opening on the side of the teepee, placed an arrow on the string of his bow and waited. When his wife stood up, he shot her through the heart with his arrow. Her laughter stopped as she fell on the teepee floor. The man with her ran out, yelling into the night. Then the husband turned and walked off into the bushes.

From that day on, whenever he heard laughter, especially in the late evening, he would follow the sound, then shoot the laughing people through the heart with his arrows. Grandmother warned us not to make too much noise, especially in the late evening when it was getting dark. We had to be quiet because that man could be out there listening for the sound of laughter. Besides him, there were other things out there in the bushes at night. We all looked at each other, wondering if the man with the bow and arrows was really out there in the bushes listening to us.

Young kids like us were scared to walk home after a storytelling session, especially after hearing stories about great medicine men and other spirit beings. Usually, we'd wait for my mother and we'd walk home with her, or we'd wait for some other woman who would drop us off at our houses on her way home.

Through stories like these, we learned how to behave or how to do certain things. From these stories, we also learned about our culture, our traditional lands, and our people.

In the winter my dad had set some rabbit snares and a few traps for squirrels and weasels (ermine) across from our village. I was six years old and I remember my mom and I would check the snares and traps when my dad was not in the village. She carried a packsack and an axe, and I followed behind. Sometimes she would pull a small toboggan and I would ride in it. I wore woven rabbit skin duffels over my socks inside my mukluks. These were soft and warm, and probably warmer than regular store-bought duffels. Grandfather wore a rabbit skin hat when he was outside getting firewood or checking his rabbit snares.

The snares we used back then were made from either moose or caribou sinew and sometimes we used store-bought twine. A piece of willow, about the size of a pencil and five to six inches long, was tied to the middle of the snare length. One end was attached to a long pole set over a large branch or over a makeshift tripod. The other end of the snare with a noose was tied to a stick in the ground. This end was tied to the stick in such a way that once a rabbit was caught, the snare would be released, causing the other end of the pole to drop, then up went the rabbit, hanging in mid air. This is how we snared the rabbits. There was no blood, no broken bones or bullet holes and the rabbits were always clean and easy to skin. There were plenty of rabbits that winter.

Sometimes I would go with my dad to check the snares and traps. I really liked going on these trips with the dog team. I would sit in the toboggan, covered with a blanket inside a large piece of canvas tarp. The toboggan also carried a gun, packsack, and pair of snowshoes. The round trip would take all day.

As we travelled along the snow-packed trail, my dad would stand at the back of the toboggan. Once in a while, he would help to push the toboggan with his foot, or run behind the toboggan to help the dogs push it up a ravine or riverbank. Sometimes I would stand at the back of the toboggan as my dad walked ahead of the dog team. I really liked doing that; it gave me a feeling of driving my own dog team.

The trail ran through an area covered with thick Jack pine trees. My dad would cut down small Jack pines or cut off branches from large ones and spread them on the snow. He said the branches would attract the rabbits, and on the next trip, we could tell if there were many rabbits in the area. The spread of branches also provided good, easy feeding for the rabbits.

I would sit in the toboggan and watch as my dad removed rabbits from the snares and reset them. I would also carefully watch him as he took a marten or lynx out of a trap and reset it. Some years later, when I was the administrator for the settlement of Fort Providence, I did some weekend trapping at my cabin about thirty miles away. There were marten, lynx and other fur-bearing animals, so I set the traps exactly as my dad had taught me years before. The price of fur, especially for marten and lynx pelts, was exceptionally high one year, so I did very well on my weekend trapping.

When we arrived at an old campfire site, we'd use snow-shoes as shovels to clear the snow and prepare to make a fire. While the fire was burning, we'd collect spruce boughs and spread them around the fireplace, taking care to place the boughs away from the wind so we wouldn't have smoke coming in our direction when we sat and ate by the fire.

Then my dad would use one snowshoe to dig down until he reached some crystallized snow close to the ground. He would put that snow in a small teapot to melt for tea. He said that this type of snow melted faster and contained more water than powder-like snow from the top of the pile. Later, we'd have some bannock and cook a fresh rabbit by the fire. While we waited for it to cook, my dad would skin a few more rabbits. He'd hang them by the fire and smoke them while we ate. Sometimes he would cook one or two more and bring them back to my mother. I remember these trips as some of the happiest and most carefree times of my childhood.

～☙～

It was during that winter that my cousins, Angie and Cathy, decided to go on a picnic in the bush across the channel from our village. They walked ahead on the trail and I followed them with a team of two dogs. Once we were across and in the bush, we came to a place where there was plenty of dried wood. Knowing this would make good firewood, they chopped some down with an axe, then chopped it into short lengths to fit my little toboggan. I helped put some of the wood into my toboggan, which must have been about five or six feet long. Once the toboggan was full, it was tied over with a length of rope.

Then looking around for a nice place to make a fire, the girls found a spot down the trail that was out of the wind. We unloaded some dried wood and made a big fire, then collected some spruce boughs and placed those around the fireplace. Then the girls made tea and cooked some fish and rabbit. After I had eaten, I started back with the dog team, pulling the toboggan loaded with firewood.

When I got to the edge of the steep riverbank, I wondered how I was ever going to get the loaded toboggan down, even with the help of the dogs pulling. The toboggan didn't hold too much wood; still, it was too heavy for me to steer properly and it was bound to tip over.

Then I remembered how the men stood at the back of their toboggans, holding on to the handles. They would keep the toboggan steady with their arms and shift their weight while steering it with one foot in the snow. This kept the toboggan upright when going down a hill or a riverbank. However, this was going to be a difficult job for a small boy like me.

The trail down the riverbank was not too long. It ran down a small ravine, but the incline of the slope was enough to give the toboggan some momentum. I got a hold of the lead dog and walked it along the trail as close as I could to the edge of the riverbank. Then I lay face down on the trail behind the toboggan and with both hands, I grabbed a good hold of the rope that held the handles. I yelled at the dogs and closed my eyes as they started to pull the toboggan down the bank, with me hanging on behind for dear life.

The snow was going up my sleeve and into my face, but I

hung on. The dog team finally stopped when it reached the ice and the trail levelled off. I was covered with snow from head to toe, but thank goodness there was nothing broken. Although it got me down the riverbank without spilling the toboggan, it was a foolish and dangerous thing to do, and I never did it again.

❧

The winter months went by, and one day when the weather got warm, my dad told us that we would be moving to a spring camp in a few days, along with the other families from our village. In preparation, my brothers helped my dad repair a sled and take it down the riverbank. The family canoe was also carried down and secured on top of the sled. It was much safer to bring them down the steep riverbank separately.

From the shed behind the house, my dad took out a gunny sack containing what I thought were small canvas bags. They were small booties for the dogs to wear to protect their paws from getting cut by sharp pieces of ice or frozen snow. Some of the booties had pieces of hide sewn to the bottom for better traction. Some had slits in the front where the dog's claws could stick out, also for better grip and traction. They were placed on each paw and held on with a piece of twine, rather than rawhide, which would only be chewed away. The dogs were useful, so everything was done to protect them as much as possible.

Early the next morning, the canoe was loaded with a tent, stove, paddles, guns and various supplies. Other families had either left or were still preparing to leave. Once all our supplies and gear were loaded, we were on the way to our spring camp. I rode in the canoe on top of the sled and my parents and brothers walked behind.

As the sun rose higher in the sky and it got warmer, we stopped every once in awhile to rest the dog teams. Then at the warmest part of the day, the dog teams were finally stopped for a long rest. The men built a big fire and the women cooked and fed us. It was just like a big family picnic. There was no hurry; the dogs needed rest and travelling would be much better in the cool of the evening.

After a good meal and a long rest, we made our way to the *K'azhaa Deh* (Horn River). Somewhere along a small channel, we stopped for the night and the tents were hastily put up around three poles, like a large tripod. This would do for sleeping and shelter for the night. The next morning, we reached the Horn River and made our way up along the shore to an area where some other families had already set up their camps.

Grandfather picked out a spot for our tents on top of the riverbank, close to a small creek. My dad and brothers cleared an area large enough for the tents, then we all sat by the fireplace and had something to eat. Over the following few days, families from the other camps began to arrive. Soon, there were many tents along the riverbank.

The snow had begun to melt and there was water in some places on the ice along the shoreline. We played outside, usually by some small puddle of water. We had small canoes carved from thick, dried, poplar bark. Sometimes we placed a small stick in the middle, attached a dried aspen leaf to it and pretended it was a sail. It really worked, especially when there was a little bit of a breeze.

Often when we played outside in the early spring months, we would take off our jackets because the sun was too warm.

Before long, my mom would call out and tell us to put our jackets back on, and when we complained that it was too hot, she would say that it was still cold and too early in the season to be running around with just a shirt on. She told us we were just inviting back the cold winter weather, so we'd quickly put our jackets back on.

I often think about this when I see young people today during the first warm days in early spring, walking around with just a shirt or a T-shirt on. Nowadays, the kids seem to be dressed for fashion, not for the weather. And if the snow and cold weather return for a few days before the spring really sets in to stay, I think to myself that they, indeed, invited back the cold weather.

As a young boy growing up on the land, I heard many stories that provided some explanation for why we must do certain things and why things were the way they were. A story was much better than an adult simply saying, "You do this because I told you so!" Children tend to listen and be a little more attentive to stories than to rules.

A few days after all the other families had arrived and the tents were set up, the men from the camp began to make preparations to leave on the annual spring hunt. The women also helped by sewing new pairs of moccasins or repairing old ones. Back then, the men used moccasins to walk in the water, so they needed more than just one pair.

The women also sewed special canvas packsacks for the dogs, so they could carry some of the supplies the men needed. The packsacks looked like miniature saddlebags that were carried on their backs and held in place with lengths of hide or canvas straps.

During spring hunts, the men carried only what they considered to be bare essentials: flour or bannock, tea, sugar, salt, guns, shells and some traps. They lived primarily off the land as they hunted and trapped beavers and muskrats. The beaver meat and other game meat was usually dried. The dried meat was much lighter to pack and move to another hunting area. When the time came to begin the hunt, the men left in twos or threes in the general direction of their traditional spring hunting areas, their dogs following behind, packing supplies. The men would be gone for three or four weeks.

As the days went by, the ice on the river slowly melted away in the warm spring sun. Once all the ice was gone, there was a run of fish. There were some elderly men in camp, like Grandfather, who went out to set fishnets. Some of the women also went out in canoes and set fishnets. In the evening, they went out again to check the nets. Soon, there was smoke coming from every outside fireplace as the women smoked and dried the fish.

During this time some of the women went out into the bush to collect birch sap. They would make a small hole in the birch tree and place a small stick into the hole. The sap would slowly flow down the stick and drip into a birchbark basket or a lard pail tied to the tree. In a day or two, the women would collect the sap and boil it until it thickened. Some would add sugar to the sap, which gave it a sweet taste.

Sometimes, Grandfather would take large pieces of bark off the spruce trees. This tree bark would be placed on the floor of the tent where it made good floor covering on top of the spruce boughs. After he removed the bark, he would gently scrape the bare part of the tree with a knife blade and collect the scrapings into a birchbark basket or some other container. We would chew the scrapings until they had no more flavour, then we'd spit them out and try some more. Sometimes, Grandmother would mix the scrapings with the thick birch sap and it tasted sweet and delicious. The sap mixture tasted somewhat like the coleslaw they once served at the Kentucky Fried Chicken restaurant in Yellowknife. But I would say our birch sap mixture tasted slightly better.

One day, Grandfather put me into a small canoe and paddled back to our village with a load of dried fish. He also brought along a .22 caliber single shot rifle, an axe and three or four small traps. He sat in the middle of the canoe and I sat immediately in front of him. A packsack, carrying a small teapot and other supplies, was placed in front of me and we were on our way. The water was high and paddling was easy.

Set back from the riverbank, there were about five log houses some distance down the Horn River at Poplar Point (*Ladze-ehda*). As we passed the houses, Grandfather paddled the canoe across the river to a small creek. Then we followed the creek, which led to the back channel, which in turn led to our village.

When we entered the back channel to Lishamie, Grandfather began to set a few traps for muskrats in the grasses and willows along the shore, close to their feeding places. Traps were set on a piece of wood and covered with grass and weeds. Twine was tied to the trap and attached to a willow or to a small, dry pole that was pounded into the riverbed, anchoring it in place. When a muskrat was caught, the trap would fall off the piece of wood into the water and drown the animal.

I sat quietly in the canoe and watched as Grandfather set the traps, learning in the same way I had done with my dad. We would pull out the traps on our way back to the spring camp.

When we arrived at our village, we had a difficult time finding a good landing spot. Some large pieces of ice had been pushed onto the shore during the breakup, and the melting ice created a muddy shoreline. We finally managed to land the canoe among some rocks, a distance down from the houses, and began to pack the bundles of dried fish up the bank to the house. Once inside, Grandfather hung the bundles from the rafters. We made a few trips up the riverbank before we had them all hanging from the rafters. By that time, it was late into the evening, so we stayed there that night. Early the next morning we paddled back to our spring camp on the Horn River.

The long, spring days passed by and it seemed like the hunters had been gone for a very long time. Then one day, we heard the sound of a gunshot from across the river. This was followed almost immediately by another shot, which echoed back into the bushes and faded.

There was excitement in the camp as some of the women ran to the shore and helped push one of the canoes into the water. A couple of them got into the canoe and paddled across the river in the general direction of the gunshots. A while later, the women returned with two of the hunters.

Over the next few days, my dad and the other men returned, loaded down with beaver and muskrat pelts and dried meat. A couple of the men returned in a small canoe made from either moose or caribou hides. The canoe was later filled with rocks and sunk so the hides would be soaked and easier to remove. The women would later work and tan the hides.

Once more, there was smoke coming from every outside fireplace, as the women began smoking and drying the meat.

Muskrat and beaver pelts were on wooden stretchers, hanging out to dry in the wind outside each tent. It seemed like there was no shortage of things we got from the land. This was a time of plenty for the entire spring camp. There were pelts, meat, ducks and fish, and no one went without.

Once the pelts had dried, most of the hunters got ready to make the trip to the settlement to trade the beaver and muskrat pelts for supplies. Some of them took dried meat and fish to sell for extra cash, with which they would buy essentials like tea, sugar, flour, tobacco and shells.

After about three days, the men returned from the settlement, each with his own store-bought supplies and a collection of stories from the settlement about what had happened over the spring period. These were mainly tidbits of news about who had visited the settlement and how well they had done during the winter and spring hunts, or news of who went away to the hospital and who had passed away.

In the evening, the men would gather at one of the tents in the middle of the camp and some would begin singing as others began to dance. There were no drums. The songs got louder as other men and women joined in the dancing. This was what we called a tea dance. It was a time of celebration and a time to give thanks for a successful spring hunt.

A few days later, some families began to move away to other camping sites. We made our way back to Lishamie, and stayed there until it was time to go and get my sister at the Sacred Heart Residential School.

Preparing to visit Lishamie

CHAPTER 3

The current was strong as the men paddled up the river towards the settlement of Fort Providence. We were on our way there to pick up my sister, Josephine, at the residential school. My mother had said it was time for my sister to come home for the summer. The river was fairly high after the spring thaw and with the annual spring run-offs from the various small creeks. There was plenty of floating driftwood and other debris, so we had to be extra careful on the river, especially in our canvas-covered canoe.

Fort Providence is situated some twenty miles or so downstream from the mouth of the Mackenzie River. At that time, it was home to the Hudson's Bay Company, the RCMP, the Signal Corps and, of course, the residential school. Lishamie was about five miles further downstream from the settlement.

The first thing to come into view as we rounded the point of Mission Island was the big, grey three-storey building. This served as the Sacred Heart Residential School, and also as the residence of the Grey Nuns and the many children in their care. The men paddled across the Snye River and up along the shore for a short distance before landing below the old Hudson's Bay store, which was the usual area for anyone who came to the settlement by canoe. Other families had already arrived and some were cooking their meals on open fires among the rocks along the shore.

As our canoe approached land, my dad asked out loud to no one in particular if the children were ready for pick-up at the residential school. One of the men on the shore replied that he had heard they would be after the Sisters had finished their noon meal. My dad nodded and then asked one of my brothers to tie up the canoe.

I remembered a few weeks back when my mother told me that I was now seven years old. I didn't know the month or day; I wasn't familiar with the English names of the months or weekdays. I only vaguely remembered my sister. I didn't know how old she was; I only knew she was my older sister. My parents would talk about her, especially after one of my dad's trips to the settlement. My mother asked if he'd had a chance to visit "our daughter", and talk of her always referred to "when your sister comes home again." I hadn't paid too much attention back then, but now I was kind of anxious as I waited in anticipation to see my sister again.

The Grey Nuns appeared very friendly, smiling and talking to some of the people, but they looked kind of strange to me. I actually thought that the nuns were born just the way they were, strange clothes and all. I also thought the priests were born the way they were, in their cassocks. It was much later that I learned they were just like you and me. But at this particular moment, the nuns scared me a bit and I stayed close to my mother.

The nuns spoke a strange language that I did not understand, but my dad spoke to them in that language. My dad later told me that it was mostly French, with some English thrown in. There were some boys and girls arriving in the visiting area and leaving with their parents when we arrived at the grey building. My dad carried on some small talk with some of the men as we waited with the other parents.

Soon, some girls arrived in the visiting area, accompanied by a Sister. A young girl came out, looked around and came straight for our family. She smiled at my mother and looked at me as we slowly walked out of the building. Once outside the residential school fence, she took my mother's hand and talked excitedly about being home for the summer. She walked with my mom a short distance then she walked back to me. She took my hand and kissed me on the forehead. I looked up at her; I was kind of shy and tried to smile, but I really did not remember her.

I often wondered why she just didn't hug my mother there in the parlour; maybe she was afraid of the Sisters, but I never did ask her about that. This was one of the many consequences of the residential school experience; after being separated from our family members for ten months or longer, we had to reacquaint ourselves with each other. It was some time later that I found out Josephine, or Josie, had been at the residential school about three years before I got there. Like most of the local students, she was able to come home for the summer months.

As we paddled our canoe back to Lishamie later that evening, my dad told me that I might be going back with my sister to the residential school in the fall. This would be confirmed when the RCMP made their usual summer patrols among the various camps to let the parents know which of their children would be going to the residential school that year. I looked at my mother as she smiled and nodded.

My dad had his fishnets set at the mouth of the channel that ran by Lishamie. It was a day or two after my sister had come home, and we were with my dad as he checked the fishnets. A large boat appeared in the distance, pushing a covered barge. From a distance, it looked just like any other tugboat that was used to transport goods to communities up and down the Mackenzie River. As it came closer, my dad told us that the boat was called the *Saint Anna,* the mission boat. It was taking some of the children from the residential school back to their parents near Jean Marie River, Fort Simpson, Wrigley, Fort Norman (now known as Tulita), Fort Franklin (now known as Deline), Fort Good Hope, and even all the way to Aklavik. The boat would make another trip in the fall to pick them up and bring them back to the residential school.

Some of the children wouldn't go home at all because there was no way for them to get there. This was especially true for the children from the Fort Liard and Nahannie Butte areas. It probably would have cost the mission a few dollars to fly them home and more money to fly them back in the fall. Some children had only their mother or only their father to look after them. In some cases, children had their grandparents or only one grandparent to look after them, so they had to spend the summer at the residential school. Whoever made these decisions, I never knew.

As the mission boat went by, we could hear the children singing *Ave Marie Stella,* a Latin hymn to the Virgin Mary, which I was later to learn and sing during masses and benediction services at the residential school. The singing faded as the boat disappeared around the bend in the river.

Back in Lishamie, there were fishnets to be checked, fish to be cleaned, water to be fetched and firewood to be collected

—everyday activities necessary for living off the land at that time. We stayed in Lishamie for a few days, then my dad said that we would be moving to the summer fishing campsite a few miles downriver. The campsite was on the south shore of Mills Lake *(Tuah)* near the place where the Big Snye flows into the Mackenzie River. Back then, there were plenty of fish and game in the area. People usually set up camps and stocked up on dried fish. The day before we moved to the fishing camp, my dad had to make a trip to the settlement for some reason and I went with him.

Paddling into Fort Providence from downriver, the first sight was the big, grey residential school building. But before this building was the priests' house, a residence for priests and Brothers. This was a large, two-storey building, complete with small single rooms on the upstairs floor. The building was used as a stopover for new priests and Brothers on their way to other communities further north.

Past the grey residential school building was the Catholic Church with its high steeple; beyond this were a couple of private homes; then the fenced-in Hudson's Bay compound with the store, warehouse and the manager's residence. Next to the fence was a small shed with forty-five gallon drums piled beside it. This was where some people bought gas and oil for their kickers. After the Bay compound, there were some more private homes; then the large fenced-in Royal Signal Corps compound; followed by about four private homes and finally the RCMP detachment compound. This was Fort Providence back in the 1950s. The only road useable for a truck ran along the riverbank from the settlement to the airstrip.

Back then, the Dene people made their living off the land and lived in permanent established camps far away from the settlement. It was only in the latter part of the 1960's that the government began to build houses and encouraged people to move to the settlement. This change in lifestyle restricted mobility, one of the basic needs of the Dene way of life. The traditional lifestyle requires the Dene to be able to move from one area to another in pursuit of game and fish. Settlement life was an abrupt change from our nomadic way of living. Later, we would see the conditions created by the transition from living off the land to settlement living.

Beyond the RCMP compound, about two miles from the settlement, was an airstrip, the local airport. Today, the airstrip doesn't seem to be two miles away. It appears closer because the settlement has expanded since the 1950s. The airstrip was built by the army during the Second World War and used as part of the staging area for supplies for the Norman Wells Canol project. The Canol project was a pipeline that was built during the Second World War from Norman Wells to the Alaska Highway, which I think was under construction at the time of the project.

When we arrived at the settlement, my dad landed the canoe on the shore at the usual place below the Hudson's Bay store. After he pulled the canoe onshore and tied it to a large rock, I followed him up the riverbank. At the store, my dad talked briefly with the clerk, and then he came out and said we had to walk over to the RCMP compound.

When we arrived, a constable greeted us at the steps of the porch door and led my dad into another room. It must have been an office of some sort. I waited in the porch by the open door and had a full view of the other room to the side. There were cupboards on the wall, a stove and a table with some chairs.

Two white men in uniforms sat by the table; they must have been from the Signal Corps compound. There were some glasses and what looked like empty bottles on the table. Back then, I'd never seen a beer bottle, nor did I know there was such a thing as beer. The two men said things to me either in French or English, which I did not understand. I just stood there and nodded or moved my head sideways to indicate a yes or a no. I don't even know what I was agreeing or disagreeing with. They sat there laughing at what must have been a big joke for them. I stood in the doorway and smiled back at them. Before long, the constable and my dad came out of the office. The constable shook hands with my dad and said something to him. Then my dad came over, took my hand and we walked out.

We headed to the Hudson's Bay store, where my dad bought a few things. Usually, he would talk with some of the people in the store, but this time he didn't say much. I followed him out of the store and down the riverbank to our canoe.

Soon, we were paddling back to Lishamie. I wasn't quite sure what, but I could sense there was something definitely wrong. My dad, who usually talked and pointed out little things of interest along the shore, didn't say too much of anything as he paddled the canoe. We arrived back home sometime in the late afternoon. My dad brought up the bag of store-bought things and put it on the ground beside my mother, who was cleaning fish by the outside fireplace. She looked up at my dad. He looked at her, shook his head and went into the house.

At once, my mother began to cry. I didn't understand why. I was scared and also started to cry when I saw my sister crying. I didn't know what was happening. My mother slowly got up and went into the house. A short while later, she came out with a small bundle of clothes. She opened the bundle and as she dropped the clothes one by one into the fire, she said in our language, "Watch over my child. Watch over my baby." Then she sat sobbing by the fireplace and whispered, "My poor little boy went away all alone among strangers."

With tears in my eyes, I walked over and stood beside her. I really didn't know what to say or do. She reached up, took my hand and I sat beside her. Then she told me that my younger brother, Philip, had passed away. He had been at the hospital in Fort Simpson. Suddenly, I remembered my dad carrying a small boy into a canoe. I think the canoe belonged to the RCMP. My dad had gone with them down the river. It seemed like such a long time ago that they had taken my little brother away to the Fort Simpson Hospital. I later learned that we had lost other family members to tuberculosis.

Being just a kid, I didn't know much about death but I wondered why people died. Then I remembered my dad's explanation of death when an elderly lady in our village passed away. She had lived next door to us with Uncle Pierre and Aunt Julie. I don't remember seeing her often in our village. She may have been bedridden. Uncle Pierre and Aunt Julie provided for her and watched over her in her old age. It was the usual custom and tradition to look after your older relatives as best you could until they passed away.

I don't recall the circumstances of her death. It may have been that she died in her sleep, maybe due to old age or some sickness. It was during the wintertime and the ground was frozen, but the men dug a grave among some tall spruce trees about one mile downstream on the bank of a point. Sometime during the day, the men returned for the body. I briefly saw the bundle of blankets that covered and wrapped her body.

This was my first glimpse of a dead person, although she was covered. The men placed her body in a toboggan and slowly took it away for burial.

Later that evening, I asked my dad what had happened to the elderly woman. My dad explained that a big owl took her away during the night. Death in itself was unexplained, like darkness. The owl, primarily a nocturnal hunter, represented danger in the night, and in this case, someone had died. This was my dad's explanation of death and nothing further was said. Death was not described as someone having died, but rather as someone being taken away. This was something I also heard several times from others as I was growing up.

⁓

At Mills Lake, there were many other tents stretched along the lakeshore. While we were at the fish camp, one of my brothers shot a moose and Grandmother worked on the hide. One day, she'd work on the hide, and the next day she was busy at something else, like making dried fish. She took her time, but before we moved camp again, she had that moose hide all tanned.

Grandmother had a large scraper, made from the limb of a moose or caribou. She used this to clean off the fleshy parts of the hide and to scrape off the hair. When this was completed, the hide was put into the water along the shore. Some of the girls from the camp helped her weight it down with rocks so it wouldn't float away. The running water cleaned the hide till it was almost white.

The hide was taken out of the water, wrung out and placed in a liquid mixture, which helped to soften it, making it easier to work with. Later, the hide was taken out of the mixture and wrung out again. With my mother on one side of the hide and Grandmother of the other side, they stretched it, pulling back and forth a number of times all around the hide. Soon, some of the girls came running over and wanted to try their hands at stretching the hide. Grandmother let them do it, as she needed a rest. The girls pulled this way and that way, and in the process, pulled each other about, laughing and having fun as they stretched the hide.

A couple of days later, Grandmother and my mother each took a packsack and went into the bush. I followed them with some of the other boys and girls. Grandmother said she was looking for a special kind of wood: some that was partially decayed. Such wood didn't catch fire easily; it just smoked and this was what she wanted – smoke to tan the moose hide. Along the way, we found some saskatoon berry bushes and we began picking and eating the berries. Meanwhile, Grandmother and my mom were busy looking for the wood, gathering several pieces and putting them into the packsacks. We grabbed a few pieces and followed them back to the camp.

The next day, the hide was temporarily sewn together for tanning. It looked like a large cylinder. My mother sewed a piece of canvas at the bottom of the hide to keep air out. If too much air got in, it would start a fire and burn the hide. My mother took turns with Grandmother and some of the girls, checking the fire under the hide, adding pieces of the decayed wood when needed. Later that evening, the hide was completely smoked and the colour was yellowish-brown. Finally, it was hung over a pole to air out.

It had been hard work, but in the end Grandmother had a beautifully tanned moose hide. My mother mentioned that she would make a new pair of moccasins for us to wear when we went to the residential school.

I remember one day there was some kind of celebration in the fish camp. Some of the young men had returned from a successful hunt, and fresh moose meat was given out to everyone. Later that afternoon, the hunters and other men from the camp began to gather at one tent and began to drink homemade brew. There was respect in the drinking back then. It was not like drinking is today, where one sits in the bar and drinks for the next few hours. The homebrew party was like a big social event. The men sat around and told stories, and there were a lot of reminiscences about special elders, childhood memories and personal experiences. There was a lot of laughter and later on, singing and dancing, carrying on into the early morning hours. This was an adult thing and we kids usually stayed away.

This was something I didn't experience very often when I was growing up. Things changed after the highway came through and people moved into the settlement from outlying traditional villages. Now there was easy access to booze. One didn't have to wait three or four days for the homebrew to go through its fermentation; one needed only to go to the bar and booze in all forms was ready and available.

Back at the summer fishing camp, people went about their daily work: getting firewood, checking their fishnets, bringing in fish, making dried fish or smoking them. Sometimes, I would hear a mother scolding her daughter who had difficulty cleaning or preparing fish for cooking. Her mother would say something like, "What did you go to the nuns' house (residential school) for? You don't even remember how to clean a fish or make dried fish. You only learned how to sign your name; what good is that?"

At that time, I didn't pay too much attention to what the mother had said. To me, she was just scolding her daughter. It was only some years later that I realized some of us children who experienced residential school living were beginning to show signs of traditional loss. It started with simple things, like the daughter not remembering how to clean fish or make dried fish. A few years of separation from our parents led to the loss of cultural and traditional values and identity, including loss of language. This is what happened to all of us who went through the residential school.

Over the next couple of weeks, the fishing activity slowed down and some individual families began to move away. Gradually, the camp emptied until there were only a few tents left. A few days later, we moved to the mouth of the channel by Lishamie. We referred to this place as Lishamie Tachee. When we arrived, my dad set up our tent in a clearing on the riverbank. A short distance upstream was my Uncle Harry's tent. Downstream and a short distance away was uncle Pierre's tent. My grandparents set up their tent at our fall fishing camp area a couple of miles further downstream and decided to wait for the coming fall fishing season. My brother, Daniel, stayed with them.

While we were at Lishamie Tachee, we would watch the riverboats go by, pushing covered barges loaded with supplies for some of the communities along the Mackenzie River. My dad and the other men seemed to recognize the boats as they came down the river. Most of the riverboat pilots were from Fort Providence. There was George's boat; I think it was called the Radium Charles. There was Vital's boat, the Pelican Rapids; Leon's boat, Jerry's boat and so on. These men would leave their homes in early spring and head to Hay River in preparation for the barging season. Once the river was clear of ice, they would pilot the first supply barges downriver. These supply boats made many trips up and down the river during the summer months.

I had a great time playing all over the bush near the tents with the other children from our camp. We played a game Grandmother showed us, a game played with a ring and a stick. The ring could be made of bone, but we used small, flexible pieces of willow branches. A length of string was tied to the stick and attached to the ring. The idea was to toss the ring and in one motion try to get the stick into the ring. When we got tired of this, we'd pound another stick into the ground and use the rings like horseshoes, trying to land the ring onto the stick.

We also played all kinds of make-believe games. We built small wigwams with dried poles and covered them with willow and aspen branches. We hung huge dried aspen leaves on sticks and made believe they were dried meat and dried fish. The girls would make small moccasins out of large aspen leaves and sew them together with grass or small, thin roots they dug from the ground. Sometimes, we'd help the girls pick large aspen leaves. We folded the leaves and bit into them. The bite marks left fancy patterns that the girls used as uppers (vamps) for their moccasins. We also dug up long, narrow willow roots from the ground. We would tie one end to a rock or a stick on the shore, then throw the length of the root into the water and pretend it was our fishnet. We also told each other stories of great hunting trips, imaginary of course, but they were good hunting stories. This was a happy and a wonderful carefree time of our childhood. We didn't know it yet, but things would change for me and the other children from Lishamie.

While we were still at Lishamie Tachee, our family tent partially burned on one side. One evening, my parents were outside cooking by the fireplace. My sister was in the tent preparing the blankets for bed. She lit a candle and put it on top of the grub box. A grub box was similar to a cooler that most people use for picnics nowadays. Back then, the grub box held some plates, utensils and other items such as sugar, coffee and tea.

When Josie shook one of the blankets, the sudden gush of air blew the candle over onto the side of the tent wall. The wall caught on fire almost instantly and began to spread to the roof of the tent. My sister yelled out as she grabbed some blankets and rushed out of the tent. My dad told me to get my Uncle Harry. I ran down the trail and yelled that our tent was burning, then ran back and saw Josie quickly rescue one of the dogs that was tied a few feet from the burning tent. The dog ran off, relieved to be away from the heat of the fire.

My Uncle Harry came running and asked if anyone was in the tent. I told him no. Just then, my dad grabbed one of the long tent poles and pulled as hard as he could. The whole tent collapsed, sending small sparks flying up into the evening air. This slowed down the fire and prevented it from spreading any further. By now, other men had come over and helped to put out the fire with pails of water.

Smoke filled the bushes, along with a very unpleasant smell of burnt canvas, but this only lasted a few moments before the wind carried it away. The tent was burnt on one side and soaked from the water that had been thrown on it. The men folded back what was left of the tent, spreading it out to dry over some willows. My mom and sister then picked up the rest of the blankets and clothing. Uncle Harry had a small tent, which he brought over and helped set up in a small clearing on the riverbank. We used that tent for a couple of weeks, while my parents sewed and repaired our burned tent.

✏

I remember there was one particularly happy occasion at Lishamie. We had all moved back to our village, and my dad and some of the other men set up a tent along the shore just below Grandfather's house. Once the tent had been set up, the women brought in spruce boughs and neatly placed them on the ground to make a floor. Later, my mother and one of the women helped another woman into the tent. Some woman built a fireplace outside, and some stayed in the tent over the next couple of days.

While this was going on, my dad and Uncle Pierre took us for long walks by the shore. Along the way, we stopped to pick and eat saskatoon berries that hung from the branches of tall bushes on the riverbank. We also threw small, dried sticks into the water and watched them float away. The men looked anxious at times, and the whole atmosphere was filled with anticipation. They did try to keep their impatience to themselves and kept busy doing things with us like, walking and skipping rocks on the water.

When we returned from one of our walks, one of the women came out of the tent and said something to my dad. Then he turned and asked us to follow him up to the tent. He and Uncle Pierre went inside as we waited outside. A short time later, my dad called and asked us to come into the tent. Curious, we all went inside and there, lying on a mat covered with blankets, was a woman; it was my Aunt Julie. In her arms was a baby covered with a small flannel blanket. We all stood there amazed, our mouths open, and wondered aloud where the baby had come from.

My mother told us that while we were away on our walk, a group of babies wandered into the camp. One of them, a little girl, came very close to the tent and the women grabbed her and put her in the blanket. "So now we have a new baby girl in our village," she explained.

This was my mother's way of telling us how the baby came to be with them in the tent. Actually, it was a beautiful story to explain to us children where babies came from. When we came out of the tent, we even looked for little footprints in the mud and sand along the shore. Some of us actually found what looked like little footprints. With some imagination, after looking hard enough at the small impressions in the mud and sand, you'd swear they were little footprints.

Boys swimming at the Snye

CHAPTER FOUR

The summer months passed quickly, and for a time I forgot about going to the residential school. The RCMP officers visited our camp during their summer patrol and had told my parents that I was scheduled to go to the residential school in the fall. I had turned seven years old in June so now, according to the police, I was old enough to go.

Early one morning, my parents loaded Josephine and me into our canoe and began paddling up the river to the settlement and to that big, grey building. I sat at the bottom of the canoe, and I was a little scared thinking about the residential school and the Sisters. I didn't know what to expect or what was expected of me. This was not just a quick visit; I was going there to stay. As we paddled on, my mind drifted back to earlier that summer and my first-ever time away from home.

My brother, Daniel, had been living with my grandparents at the fishing camp downriver. He had been spending more time looking after and caring for Grandfather and Grandmother since Archie had married and moved away. Daniel was a practical person, like my dad, and did things that needed to get done. He was good to me and I liked being with him. He showed me how to set fishhooks through the ice at early freeze-up, and we'd catch a type of catfish we called *loche*.

One summer day, I went with him to collect firewood. On our return back to camp, we heard someone whistling at us from the bushes. I had heard stories about the boogeyman who kidnapped children, and immediately thought we were in grave danger. I was really scared and on the verge of crying, but Daniel told me to calm down and act naturally. He was carrying a load of wood on his shoulders and put it down on the trail. We heard the whistle again. Daniel slowly took the axe out of the packsack and told me to keep on walking. Suddenly, we heard laughter and someone shouted, "Hey!" We looked back to see a man and a boy come out of the bushes. They had been hunting rabbits, but they had also certainly done a good job of scaring me. I realized then that Daniel was prepared to defend me against any danger, even to the point of fighting with a boogeyman.

So when Daniel paid our family a visit that summer, I asked my parents if I could go back with him and stay with my grandparents for a few days. They agreed, so I set off early the next morning with Daniel on my first adventure away from my parents. It was going to be fun, I thought. As my brother paddled, I sat at the front of his small canoe and we travelled quickly downstream with the current, arriving in no time at my grandparents' camp.

I spent the rest of the day helping around the camp. Daniel and I helped Grandfather stretch a fishnet between two poles along the shore. Then he went about checking the net for tears and mending them. I walked the length of the stretched fishnet looking for tears, and when I found one, I'd tie a piece of grass onto the tear so Grandfather could find it and mend it. In the evening, after we had our meal, I walked with Daniel to the river to get a couple pails of water. Then Daniel chopped some wood and I carried it back into the tent.

As evening began to set in, Grandmother put some blankets together and made a place for me to sleep next to Daniel. I lay down on the blankets and looked at the ceiling of the tent, trying to settle in for the night. I was all right at first, but soon I started thinking about my parents and I began to feel homesick. Then I began to cry.

After awhile, Grandmother asked me what was wrong. I just mumbled that I wanted to go home. She came over and held my head on her lap trying to comfort me. I just kept on crying. "Shh-shh-shh," she whispered, rocking me gently and stroking my hair. "Grandfather is trying to sleep."

Finally after some time, Grandfather—probably out of frustration and desperation—called out to my brother and told him to take me home. It was late summer and just enough daylight to see the shoreline. Daniel put me in the canoe and didn't say much as he paddled upriver, staying close to the shore. The trip back was tougher against the current, and Daniel had to really push. He sure wasn't too happy about taking me home, especially at night, and I heard him mumbling angrily under his breath.

When we arrived back at my parent's camp, my dad asked what had happened. Daniel explained the situation to him as best he could and asked if he could stay for the night. While they were still talking, I went into the tent, crawled into some blankets and went directly to sleep in a warm, comfortable, familiar place.

That was my first experience being away from my parents and home. I thought of the residential school and wondered what was going to happen once my parents walked away from that place, leaving me there.

The canoe drifted close to the shore and we landed at the usual place below the Hudson's Bay store. My sister Josephine and I got out of the canoe and sat with my mother on the rocks by the shore. My dad took his time tying up the canoe. Once the canoe was secured, we followed our parents up to the top of the riverbank where other parents had gathered with their children. Next, they took us to the Hudson Bay store nearby and bought us some candies. Then they stopped and talked to other parents.

I knew our parents were trying to delay our inevitable separation from them, but it was just a matter of time before we joined other families walking toward the big, grey building. My sister and I walked with our mother as she held our hands, following our dad who was carrying our bags.

I didn't want my parents to think that I was afraid, so I pretended to be anxious to get there. In a show of bravado, I said that I could jump over the fence and play with the other kids who were already there. We walked past the big church, then along the hedge-covered fence and to the gate in front of the residential school. A short sidewalk led to a wide staircase, which in turn led up to the front door. My dad rang the door-bell as we all stood close together. The door to the parlour area opened and we walked in.

I wasn't afraid up to this point, but the sudden appearance of the Sisters did frighten me. Before I could think, my mother let go of my hand and the Grey Nuns guided me through into the parlour. The reality hit me: I was being taken away from my parents! I started crying and tried to hang onto the door frame as the Sisters pulled me away. Trying her best to soothe me, my mother kept promising she would come back and visit us soon. By this time, my sister had already been led away. She had been here before and knew what was expected of her, so she picked up her bag and followed one of the Sisters to the girls' section of the building. I'm sure she heard my cries and screams of protest.

I soon realized that I could have carried on screaming until my throat was hoarse and it wouldn't have made a bit of difference to the Sisters. They knew sooner or later I would resign myself to the fact that I was there to stay. It troubles me to remember how the Grey Nuns seemed to be very indifferent to the presence of my parents as they took me away. My parents were powerless to do anything; it was simply the way things were. It was the law.

I imagine the whole experience was very hard on my parents as they watched their children being taken away, and treated roughly in the process. It must have been especially hard for my mother, and it probably broke her heart to see us like this and be unable to help us.

One of the Sisters grabbed my bag and rushed ahead down the hallway. I saw my mom and dad standing there as the doors closed behind me. I was now alone with strangers in a strange, big house, and I didn't understand their language.

I spent my first day at the residential school with the other new boys. Some of us were silent and scared, with tears in our eyes and not knowing what to do. Some of the other boys were sobbing uncontrollably. The two Sisters who were supervising the boys gathered us on the first floor of the building in a large room with benches along the walls. This was the boys' recreation room. From there, we were led in single-file upstairs to a large dormitory on the second floor and were each assigned to a bed. One of the older boys, who had been through the residential school before, acted as our interpreter. We were told to undress, put our clothes on our bed and get ready for a bath.

Once in the bathtub, the Sister poured a green-coloured liquid onto our heads and bodies, and we washed ourselves. Our clothes and other personal belongings were taken away and we were all given denim coveralls. We were to wear these at play and at work for the duration of our stay at the residential school.

Some years later in high school, I saw a documentary film about the Third Reich, showing Jews arriving at a concentration camp. The Jews appeared very passive; they didn't fight back. It seemed they understood that it was their fate and they accepted that fact. The Jews all stood in single file as they were separated from their loved ones. Then their clothes, suitcases, and other personal belongings were taken away. Finally some were given "showers".

The whole movie scene was eerily similar to what we went through at the residential school, and some scenes would bring back memories of my time at the big, grey building. A word, a name, a certain smell: these would later stir memories of the residential school and at times haunt my dreams. This is one of the consequences of the whole residential school experience.

The Sisters who supervised the boys spoke mostly French and very little English. We, the newcomers, spoke only Slavey and understood neither French nor English. The only way to communicate was through interpretation by an older boy who understood the Sisters' language.

After our baths, we got dressed and were put into single file again. Then we followed the Sister downstairs to the recreation room on the first floor, where we were told to wait. I had been crying off and on for some time now and I sat with the rest of the boys on a long bench. I had my head down looking at the floor. Once in a while, I'd look at the door, hoping my dad would come into the big room and take me home. Oh, how I desperately wished he could just come in and do exactly that.

While we waited for the Sisters, I could hear some of the other new arrivals still sobbing or trying to catch their breath. When the Sisters returned, one of them motioned for us to get into a single file again. Then we followed the other Sister out of the room and downstairs to the basement level for supper.

The dining room was a large, open area. A piano or organ sat against the wall in the middle of the room. This more or less indicated the separation point between the boys' and girls' dining areas. The girls' designated dining area was on one side of the room and the boys' area on the other. We sat on benches at long tables. I looked up as the girls entered their dining area and tried to catch a glimpse of my sister, but I didn't see her. I returned my gaze to the enamel plate in front of me on the table. That enamel plate also served as a bowl for soup and porridge. I couldn't eat much because I had a lump in my throat. I kept thinking of my parents, getting very homesick, and I started to cry again. The Sisters didn't pay too much attention to me at that time, maybe because I was new to the ways of the residential school. They also knew I was there to stay no matter what.

After supper, we all stood up and said grace, just like we had done before supper. Once again, I didn't understand what was being said. I was to learn and memorize this meal prayer both in French and English. Later on, we even sang grace in French before meals. Whether we said grace or sang grace depended on the whim of the Sister supervising at mealtime.

Bedtime that first evening was the hardest for me. I was used to sleeping an arms' length from my dad. But tonight I would sleep alone in a strange place and it scared me. The dormitory was not that big, but to a small, seven-year-old, it was huge and intimidating. The walls and the ceiling of the dormitory appeared to be very high, much higher than the walls of our log house back home. It was a big change from our log house in Lishamie to the nuns' big house.

There were about four rows of beds in the dormitory. At one end was the wash area with sinks and small mirrors that hung on one wall. There were a few windows and just one door that led out of the dormitory onto the stairway. Not understanding the language and not wanting to get into any trouble, I watched the other boys and did as they did. Once again the boys said prayers out loud, and this time we all knelt by our beds. I didn't know any prayers, not in French or English anyway, so I just bowed my head and looked at the floor.

After everyone was in bed, the Sister turned out the lights, except for one small light in the corner of the wash area. It was almost dark and I was scared. I wrapped the blankets around me and covered my head. Thinking of my parents and wondering when I was going to see them again, I started to cry again. Not wanting to attract attention to myself, I cried under the blankets with my hand over my mouth. Eventually I fell asleep.

The next morning, we were awakened by one of the Sisters, who was clapping her hands together and telling us in a loud voice to get out of bed. Still afraid and not wanting to cause any trouble, I got out of bed immediately. After washing up, we got into single file and went downstairs to the dining area for a breakfast of porridge, beans and bread. From this day on, my life was to be governed by a clock. There was a certain time to eat; time to go to school; time to go to mass; time to go to bed; time to get out of bed; time to play; time to do chores, and so on. Back home, we ate whenever we were hungry, not because the clock said twelve or six.

This day also introduced me to the rules and regulations of the residential school; rules that I had to obey and abide by at all times. Those who broke the rules were punished in several ways. I was placed into a very strict and regimented system, a lifestyle which was not like the relaxed family environment I was used to back home. It was for all of us newcomers, a culture shock. This type of regimented lifestyle was more in keeping with a religious life meant for priests and nuns, or a prison life meant for convicts.

After breakfast, we, the newcomers, sat on benches along the walls and watched some of the boys, busy doing their chores. The boys were assigned certain duties, like sweeping the stairs, washing the sinks, cleaning the washrooms, and so on. Everyone was busy doing this and that, and as each chore was completed, the boys would sit on the benches with us and wait. When all the chores were done, everyone went to their assigned classrooms, either upstairs or downstairs. The newcomers were the exception; we had to wait for the Sister to take us to our classroom. When the Sister arrived, we followed her upstairs. Our classroom was one floor above the boys' dormitory. So began my very first day of school at the Sacred Heart School.

I was assigned a desk, which had a hole in one corner. I learned the hole on the desktop was called an inkwell, designed to hold a small bottle of ink. But it would be some time before we would have an ink bottle on our desk. First we had to learn to read and write.

For the first few days of school, communication was very difficult for me as I didn't speak or understand English or French. It took some time before I learned enough to be able to speak and understand some English. Soon after that, we were forbidden to speak Slavey. The Sisters probably thought we would learn English faster, or maybe they thought we were talking about them when we spoke our language. It seems ironic when I think about it now, because the Sisters who supervised us at that time spoke only French; they didn't speak English that well. As a consequence, we learned broken English from them.

Not being able to speak my own language really created a communication problem for me. It was especially hard when my parents came to visit us. I wasn't quite sure if the restriction applied when speaking to my own parents. I did speak to them in our language only after I was sure the Sisters weren't around or close by. Like most people in Fort Providence at that time, my dad spoke French fluently. He also spoke some English. But he always spoke to us in South Slavey when he came to visit us. I don't think he was aware of the language restriction, and I never did tell him about it.

I remember one day during class, one of the Sisters brought a young girl, maybe six or seven years old, into the classroom. The Sister then said to the other, "Look, listen to this." Then she said something in English to the young girl and asked her to repeat the sentence in South Slavey. The young girl did as she was told and translated the sentence, much to the delight of the Sister. She thought it was just great to have such a young girl who understood English and South Slavey. It appeared like a great novelty to her.

In the classroom, most of the other kids were my age: six or seven years old. The Sisters taught us how to say the alphabet and numbers. It was a repetitive process that we went through every day until we were able to recognize the letters and numbers. Back home, we learned by watching and remembering how to do things, but the Sister's way of teaching was to pound it into you until you learned it.

When we were able to read, the Sister gave us a book to read in class. It was about a boy named Dick, a girl named Jane and their dog, named Spot. We would "see Dick jump; see Jane run; and hear Spot go bow-wow." It sure was a strange little book for me because I never heard my father's dogs go "bow-wow" when they barked. When I read about Dick and Jane, immediately I visualized a house on a street someplace far away. Not necessarily someplace down south, but just far away. The one pictured in the book showed a paved street with quaint little houses and a neat row of trees. This was something you wouldn't find around Fort Providence in the 1950s. You certainly won't find that today, either.

The Sister also taught us songs like *Old MacDonald Had a Farm; A Drummer Boy from War Came Marching Gaily; Little Bo Beep; Mary Had a Little Lamb; Three Blind Mice; Row, Row, Row Your Boat,* and so on. These were all totally strange songs and not what I was accustomed to.

Later on, besides the ABCs and 1-2-3s, we learned and memorized some prayers. The entire school curriculum was naturally based on reading and writing, but with a heavy emphasis on religion. I think actual education came second. The school system did not train any of us for life careers or employment. It was not geared to prepare the kids for future careers or to pursue higher education after the residential school. We just went to school to read and write and, of course, to be good Catholics. That was it.

I remember one day in class, the Sister asked us to write down what we wanted to be when we grew up. I wrote down that I wouldn't mind being an airplane pilot. We had watched the pilots land their planes on the river in the summer and on the frozen ice at the Snye in the winter. It looked exciting, and it certainly gave a person an opportunity to see different parts of the country. When we finished, we placed our papers on the Sister's desk as we left the classroom.

The next afternoon, the Sister asked me to stay after class. I thought I had done something wrong and I was a little apprehensive. After the other kids were gone, she called me over to her desk. I walked over and stood there, looking down at the floor. I waited for some kind of scolding but to my surprise and relief, she asked if I really wanted to be an airplane pilot. I replied that I thought I could be one, if I was given the chance to learn what was required to fly a plane. She told me that I would have to go to school for a very long time.

Then she told me that some of the other kids said they wanted to be a priest, a Brother or a Sister. Did I ever think about becoming a priest or a Brother? The thought had never once crossed my mind, and I didn't want to tell her that so I didn't say anything. I didn't want her to be angry with me. I just shrugged my shoulders and looked at the floor. She said that maybe I really should think about what I wanted to be when I grew up.

I think most of the other kids wrote down that they wanted to be a priest, a Brother or a sister just to please the Sister. I don't think any one of them had the slightest intention of following through with their plans. I never became a pilot, and most of those kids are working at various jobs. All of them are now parents and some are grandparents. So much for religious life after the residential school.

After school, we'd change into our coveralls and if the weather was nice, we played outside until we were called in for supper. Some days the Sister would tell us to bring in some wood for the kitchen. Dividing the boys' and girls' yards was a chicken coop inside a high fenced-in yard. Next to the chicken coop were long rows of cordwood, about five or six feet high. The wood had been cut to length for the kitchen stove and the boiler. The Brothers had a constant fire going under the boiler producing hot steam for the radiators, especially during the winter. These radiators stood under most windows and in some corners of the building, which kept it warm during the long, cold winter months.

We brought in the wood, one armload at a time or on our small sleds, and threw it down a small chute to the floor of the boiler room. Other boys were down there separating the wood, piling it in rows according to length. They placed long pieces of wood for the boiler against one wall, and short pieces for the kitchen against the other wall. Bringing in the wood became a regular chore, especially during the wintertime.

The Sisters looked after the chickens, and the Brothers looked after the cows and horses. There were times when we had to clean out the chicken coop and the barn. The horses were used mainly to haul the firewood. In the spring and fall, they were used to plow the potato fields. The horses were also used to haul in wagonloads of hay in the fall from a place we called the Mission Prairie.

There was a high, wooden slide next to the fence in the boys' yard. On the other side of the fence was the big, log barn. One day, as we were playing on the slide, we noticed one of the Brothers come out of the barn leading a cow. We stopped playing and watched with curiosity as he led the cow to the back of the barn. Soon, other boys joined us on the deck of the slide to watch.

At the back of this log barn were two large openings that led into what looked like a large, high-ceiling garage. In the fall, the Brothers drove a wagon filled with hay into this opening and threw the hay up into the loft with long-handled pitchforks. As we watched, the Brother threw some hay on the ground for the cow. Almost immediately, it took a mouthful and began to chew. The Brother tied the cow to a large, wooden beam running across the floor of the opening.

Then, he walked to the wall at the far end of the opening and came back with an axe. The cow was contentedly chewing away on the hay, oblivious to what was about to happen. The Brother stood beside the cow, lifted the axe over his head and swung it down with all his might. The flat part of the axe landed squarely on the cow's forehead and it went down. After a short while, another Brother arrived to help with the cow. He grabbed a length of chain from one of the pulleys hanging from the rafters and put a hook under the cow's chin. Together, they strung up the cow, then closed the big barn doors and left.

We continued playing until the Brothers came back pushing a small wagon. We stopped and watched them again. One of the Brothers placed a large tub under the cow, then they started skinning it and taking out its innards. The cow's warm body gave off a fog-like mist that rose up to the rafters as the

Brothers cut up the meat. They strung up the limbs and ribs on hooks that hung from the rafters.

A while later, one of the Brothers walked up to the fence and called us over to help put the meat into the wagon. The cow meat looked a little pale; it was not red like moose or caribou meat. We helped the Brothers push the wagon a short distance to a cellar-like shed that had been built into the bank of the ravine and covered over with dirt. Grass and other shrubs had grown over the top so it was not visible until you were right upon it. Near the corner of the shed was a thick wooden door. I don't know how big the shed was but I remember the floor was covered with sawdust. The one small light bulb barely lit up the room. In the dim light, we could see some large pieces of ice on the floor; some parts of it were also covered with sawdust. Other meat hung from hooks along the wall; some of it was most likely moose meat. The Brothers put the fresh cow meat on some hooks hanging from the wooden beams of the shed and we left.

This was my first experience watching someone actually kill a cow and butcher it. I had watched my dad and other men skin a moose, caribou or a bear, but this was something really different. The Brothers didn't have to hunt, track down and shoot the cow. It was already waiting in the barn. There was no hardship in hunting and finding the game.

I also remember watching one of the Brothers as he grabbed some chickens by the legs and chopped off their heads. The headless chickens would bounce around the yard until they were finally still. Then the Brother would put them into a gunnysack and take them to the kitchen. I never did see the girls or Sisters in the kitchen actually clean the chickens. Eventually, we did have some beef or chicken for some of our meals. Usually, it was served in the form of a stew or soup, nothing too exotic. I guess the choice parts had been fed to the priests, Brothers and Sisters.

Planting potatoes in the spring.

CHAPTER FIVE

The physical barriers separating the boys' and girls' yards were the rows of wood by the chicken coop. The other barrier, unseen but understood, was the aisle between the girls' and boys' dining areas. There were times when I wanted to see or talk to my sister, Josie, but I wasn't allowed to talk to her and I only saw her from a distance during meal times. I couldn't even acknowledge her with a simple nod or a smile to indicate I was all right because I was afraid of the Sisters.

I remember one of the Sisters used to shake some unfortunate boy by the neck with both of her hands until he would be crying. This was her form of punishment for what she saw as bad behavior. I wasn't about to subject myself to such treatment so I tried very hard not to provoke such action. But being only seven years old, like most kids, I did get into trouble. Most of the time it was an innocent mistake, however, because there were rules to follow that we never knew about or understood. For the first few months at the residential school, we learned these rules the hard way.

One day while I was home for the summer holidays, I went with one of my brothers on a duck-hunting trip on the river. He'd shoot the duck, and grab it as they floated by the canoe.

If a duck was still alive, he'd wring its neck and throw it into the canoe. Immediately, I would remember the Sister at the residential school shaking some poor boy by the neck. There was one particular Sister who, once annoyed or angry, would look sternly in the direction of the perceived troublemaker. She would stand there with her arms bent at the elbows, like a gunslinger just before a gunfight in a western movie. If she came at you in this particular posture, you knew you were in for some neck shaking. While she shook you, she would say, "*tien, tien, tien.*" I didn't know what it meant; I just thought it was some swear word used only by the nuns. Like the other boys I wasn't immune to this kind of treatment; I did get my share of this punishment a number of times during my stay at the residential school.

As the residential school was a Roman Catholic establishment, there were religious services almost every day and for all kinds of occasions. I learned some prayers by heart, like the Hail Mary, the Lord's Prayer, the Apostles' Creed and others. I memorized these prayers but I never understood what they meant or why we recited them; therefore I did not feel any profound religious emotion as I said them. I merely learned and memorized these prayers because it was demanded of me by my religious supervisors and teachers. At the age of seven, I had no concept of religion, and the missionaries were not sensitive to the culture of the local Dene people. Their religion was imposed upon us, they believed, for our own good.

Along with prayers, I also learned some Latin hymns by heart. These were sung at masses, benediction services and other special occasions. Again, I didn't understand a word, but I memorized these Latin hymns and sang along with the other kids in church. These hymns sounded a lot like some of the

Gregorian chants we hear once in a while on the radio, TV and even in the movies.

Before long, I was memorizing the Act of Contrition and going to confession in preparation to receive my first communion, and I was still only seven years old. At our first communion, the boys wore special black blazers with narrow banners over our shoulders that were made from some kind of red satin cloth. The banners were like wide straps with gold-coloured borders and gold-coloured tassels that hung at the end. The girls wore white dresses and white veils that covered their heads. After the service, we gave all the blazers and banners back to the Sister, and they were put away for the next group of boys who would receive their first communions or confirmations.

I always thought that the priests and sisters were never wrong, because they did things in the name of God. We were taught that the Pope was the head of the Catholic Church and that he was infallible. I never questioned anything, nor was I given an opportunity to question anything. I was never given the encouragement to look at something beyond its present state. What I mean is that I didn't get the chance to ask, "What if?" or "What does it mean?" I just had to believe.

There were times when the Sisters would send us all into the chapel to go to confession, whether we wanted to or not. This was usually on a Saturday, or the day before some special occasion. I'd go into the confessional, but sometimes I really had nothing to tell the priest. I would make up some stories just so I had something to tell him. In so doing, I sinned by confessing to some sins I never committed in the first place. Come to think of it, the whole situation was pretty bizarre.

A typical day at the residential school began at approximately six o'clock in the morning. One of the Sisters would wake up the boy who was assigned to serve as an altar boy at the early mass that morning. At about six-thirty, the same Sister would wake up the other boys assigned to serve as altar boys at the second mass, which began about seven o'clock. Some of the other boys would get up at that time to go to mass if they wanted to. On special occasions during the week, such as the feast of a special Saint, or the birthday of the Pope or Bishop, or the birthday of the Father Superior or Sister Superior, we would all get up to go to mass, like it or not.

After the morning mass, we had breakfast at about eight o'clock, usually porridge and bread or beans and bread. On special occasions, such as Christmas or Easter, we would get corn flakes and milk, sometimes with toast. After breakfast, we did our assigned chores and then go to school.

At lunchtime, we usually had soup and bread or buns. Sometimes it included leftovers from last night's supper or leftover beans from breakfast. After lunch, it was back to school until about three-thirty, at which time we all went back into the recreation area and changed into our one-piece coveralls. Sometimes, the Sister would give us a bun or a carrot for a snack, especially if we were about to work hauling wood for the kitchen and boiler room. The odd time we just played outside until supper was ready.

Supper was the biggest meal of the day, and usually consisted of fish or meat stewed with potatoes and some bread. Sometimes, when there were leftover potatoes, the Sister would get some butter and spread it over them. Butter was something we rarely got, so it was a treat. The buttered potatoes tasted a lot better than just plain old potatoes.

The priests and Brothers had their meals in a separate enclosed dining room on the same floor as our dining area. The

Sisters also had their own dining room next to the kitchen area. The girls usually served the meals to the priests and Brothers. They would pass by our tables pushing a cart with covered dishes containing food, and I'm sure, it was not like what we were being fed.

One day, we were served some kind of soup that was like gruel; it consisted of some broth with clear balls, like little marbles, floating around in it. These looked like tapioca seeds. I tried a spoonful but it tasted strange and I just couldn't swallow it. It made me want to throw up. So when no one was looking I spit the soup back into my plate. The other boys were eating their soup, but for some reason, I just couldn't eat it.

After awhile, the Sister noticed me. She walked over and asked why I wasn't eating my soup. I tried to explain to her as best I could why I couldn't eat it. Then she told me that I wasn't getting anything else until I finished all of my soup. I had my head over the plate with another mouthful, desperately trying not to throw up. The Sister moved beside me, plainly getting very impatient. Once in a while, she would hit my arm or my shoulder with the soup ladle she had in her hand. Even though the punishment was painful, I would not swallow the soup because I was afraid I might throw up. She reminded me of the German officer in the Holocaust film documentary, who carried a special rod as a sign of authority.

Suddenly, the Sister hit my hand with the soup ladle, and at the same time my hand hit the edge of the plate and splashed the soup onto the table and floor. The enamel plate bounced off the bench and crashed onto the floor, sending the clear little marble-like balls rolling in all directions. I also spit out whatever soup I had left in my mouth. This infuriated her and she hit me again across the hand with the soup ladle. I started to cry and looked up at the other boys. They moved away from the table as if to make room for the Sister.

This was my first abusive incident with the Sisters since arriving at the residential school. I continued crying, not knowing what to do. There was no place for me to run to and hide. The whole situation seemed impossible and hopeless to me. Even if I could defend myself, it didn't seem like the proper thing to do. I had to take whatever was coming. There was no one to go to for help and no one around to console or comfort me. I felt alone and completely helpless.

When I remember this incident, it reminds me again of the Jews in the concentration camps. They were very passive in the midst of all that cruelty. They even ran into the ditches where they were shot. We were also passive, not reacting to the treatment we received at the hands of the Sisters. I often wonder about that in my later years—why did we not defend ourselves against this kind of treatment? Maybe it would have been regarded as a sin to defend ourselves or retaliate against our religious supervisors for the harsh treatment.

I don't think the Sisters were trained in child-care or in bringing up a child. Their concern was strictly religious and had nothing to do with human values, or with comforting and caring for someone else. At times like this, I really missed my parents. I knew they wouldn't have treated me like that or have done such things to me. Sometimes I cried, saying under my breath, "*Aba*" (Father) or "*Ama*" (Mother) in my language. Just calling out to them brought some measure of comfort to me.

The Sister stood by me with the ladle in her hands and watched as I cried and cleaned up the mess. Finally, she took my plate and ordered me upstairs to bed. When I got to the dormitory, I got into bed as quickly as I could. Then I waited in anticipation for more scolding from the Sister but she never came. I fell asleep and later woke to the noise of the rest of the boys as they came upstairs for bed. I was awake but had my eyes closed and just lay in bed. Then all was quiet as the Sister put out the dormitory lights.

After this incident with the Sister, I was always careful about what I did. For a long time, actually until I left the residential school, I did things I was told to do immediately. I learned to do this so I wouldn't get into any trouble with the Sisters. In this way, I hoped they would leave me alone. Inevitably though, there were times when something would go wrong, something I did not know that I did, but it resulted in me being punished just the same.

One morning, the Sister woke us all up in her usual fashion, clapping her hands and telling us to get out of bed. Some of the boys had already made their beds and had gone to Mass. We were the last ones to get out of bed that morning; we didn't have to go to Mass.

This particular morning, one of the boys, Tommy, had wet his bed. The Sister was furious. She ordered Tommy to kneel on the floor by his bed. Then she walked over and slapped him behind the head. He began to cry as he knelt there. Then the Sister ordered him to collect his bedsheet and blankets, and had him stand in the corner by the bathtub.

We all slept in our underwear, a one-piece that we called long-johns. The boy quickly took them off and the Sister had him drape the wet long-johns around his shoulder as he stood by the bathtub. This was not only physical abuse; it was mental abuse. Tommy was humiliated. It was chilly in the dormitory, and the boy was crying and shivering with the wet long-johns draped over his shoulders.

We all continued dressing and washing up as this whole episode took place in front of us. We didn't do anything. No one came forward in the boy's defense. It would have been a different story if this had happened back home. But here, there was really nothing any of us could do. No one dared to do anything. We watched and got in line as usual in preparation to go downstairs for breakfast.

The Sister finally came over to the boy and ran cold water in the bathtub. Still crying, Tommy removed his wet long-johns from his shoulders and got into the bathtub. He washed himself as the Sister stood by, prodding him with the handle of a scrubber to hurry him up. When he was done, he dried himself, then slowly made his way back to his bed and put on his clothes.

Then the Sister told him to wash his wet long-johns, the sheet and blankets in the same water he just washed himself in. When he was done washing them, he brought them outside and hung them on the clothesline. It was during the winter and his long-johns and blankets froze stiff on the line. Sometime during the day, he was told to bring them in and take them to the dormitory to dry out.

I knew Tommy. He never wet his bed when he was home with his parents. I guess the residential school affected each of us in different ways.

⸎

On Sundays, the day would begin as usual with the Sister clapping her hands to wake us up. However, then after breakfast and chores, we got ready for the High Mass, which began about ten o'clock in the morning. The Sunday High

Mass was held in the chapel of the residential school during the winter and in the big church during the spring and summer months. The big church was also used for mass on special occasions, such as Christmas and Easter. This was to accommodate the people who came into the settlement from their camps and villages.

My first time in the big church was at a Sunday High Mass. To me, as a small boy, the church appeared to be very large and spacious. There were tall pillars that seemed to hold up the high dome ceiling. At the back of the church was a balcony that was used by the choir. The balcony reminded me of a loft in a cabin. There was also an organ near the balcony railing. Down on the church floor, there were rows of pews. There was a wide aisle in the middle and two other narrow ones close to the walls. The confessional compartment was under the balcony on one side of the main door. On the other side of the main door was a small room with benches against the wall.

After High Mass, we went back to the recreation area, changed into our coveralls and had lunch. After lunch, we had an hour or two for playtime. We either played inside or outside, depending on the weather and on the whim of the supervising Sister. Later in the afternoon, the Sister called us in and we got ready for benediction service. This service consisted of hymns, the rosary and the priest blessing the people with the consecrated host in the monstrance.

The monstrance was shaped in the form of a cross, with what appeared to be rays of light emitting from its centre. In the centre of the cross was a circular opening covered with glass on either side. Inside this glass was the consecrated host. One of the altar boys would ring the bells and the people bowed their heads as the priest, holding up the monstrance, blessed them. This same service was conducted every Sunday afternoon and sometimes in the evenings during the week. After supper, our Sunday ended with the usual playtime, prayer time and finally, bedtime.

Sundays were supposed to be a day of worship, and all other activities were forbidden. Back in Lishamie, I remember an incident one Sunday afternoon when a man was walking among the tents, asking someone to give him a haircut. He even had a pair of scissors and a comb. Then someone told him that such a thing was forbidden, and potentially sinful, on Sundays. Things like haircuts, hauling wood, hauling water, and even cutting fingernails were not done on Sundays. Sunday was a day of rest and everyone was expected to go to church. This was the kind of thinking that people had back then; it was instilled through the teachings of the priests.

At school, besides Dick and Jane, 1-2-3s and A-B-Cs, we learned some history, arithmetic, science, and, of course, we had a daily half-hour or so of catechism. The Sister gave each of us each a booklet, which contained religious questions and answers. We were required at times to memorize some of these questions and answers. This was done especially when one was preparing for first communion or confirmation. The priest-in-charge, the Father Superior, or one of the other priests taught catechism. Sometimes, the religious lessons were taught by one of the Sisters if the priest was unavailable.

Here is where I first learned about sin. I was old enough to know the difference between good and bad deeds, just like I knew the difference between good and bad weather, or good and bad food. However, I had no concept of sin until I learned about it from the priest during catechism lessons. I think most of the Dene people had no concept of sin as such, until the priests, Brothers and Sisters arrived. They were the ones who introduced us to the idea of sin and described other activities they considered to be the evils of life. I think we were doing all right until the missionaries arrived.

We learned about mortal sin and the original sin, and we were taught that we were all born with the original sin. The only way to get rid of this sin was to be baptized into the Catholic faith. Otherwise when you died, your soul would be stuck in limbo for eternity. This was my understanding of what we were taught during catechism lessons.

I often wondered about the old people and babies who had died long before the missionaries arrived among us. What had happened to the souls of those people? Did they all go to hell because they weren't baptized? These questions played on my mind, and I assumed it played on the minds of the other boys, too. But we never asked because we were afraid to question; we just had to learn and believe.

All things and actions not directly related to God were considered potentially sinful. There were times when I found myself trying to be very careful in what I said or did, in case I committed a sin. I remember there was a large poster that hung on the wall in the classroom; the same poster also hung in the dining area and on other walls in the residential school building. It showed a road to heaven with pictures of all kinds of people. There were other roads branching off from the main road. I imagined this indicated sinning and straying from the righteous path.

The illustration also showed purgatory, where people stopped to do penance and to be purified before continuing on to heaven. There were people stuck in limbo because they were never baptized, and still some others were burning in hell. The poster depicted the devil as an evil-looking character with horns protruding from his forehead, holding a large pitchfork, his feet curled and wrinkled. I guess that's where the South Slavey word for devil came from. *Eke tseli* in South Slavey literally means wrinkled foot. This is what the people saw in pictures of the devil, and this is the name that was given to him.

I don't think there was a name for the devil in the South Slavey language until the missionaries introduced him in their attempts to convert the people. There were stories of evil spirits, but they were not given names. The missionaries probably showed us the picture of the devil to describe an evil person. So besides praying and trying to be good, we would be tempted by Old Wrinkled Foot for the rest of our lives.

We were taught many things, including the belief that the Catholic religion was the true universal religion. One day, as part of the industrial arts class, we went with the Sister to watch the Brothers work on an old, red truck. One of the Brothers named off some of the engine parts—or at least he tried. His English wasn't that good, but the Sister helped him along. He pointed to some parts like the spark plugs, alternator, battery, carburetor and the universal joint. As soon as he mentioned the word 'universal,' immediately I thought of the universal religion and wondered what the difference was between the two of them.

Sometimes, I think we were just like little ducklings that had things imprinted in their minds. The priests and Sisters probably thought that this kind of learning would make us act in the proper and righteous ways, so they tried hard to instill these beliefs in us. It was an attempt to change our actions to fit in with their own concept of what they regarded as proper and righteous behaviour.

According to the priests who taught us, it was blasphemous to say anything derogatory about the church or about the priests. This was because they did the bidding of the church in accordance with papal enunciation or proclamations.

One day, the Sister was teaching one of the catechism classes when the Father Superior walked into our classroom. He looked over us with a stern expression on his face and closed the door. His face was red and he was visibly upset and angry about something. He had a folded piece of paper in his hand, which he shook and held up for us to see.

He told us that it was a letter, written by one of the girls to her friend. It contained things that shouldn't be written to anyone or about anybody. He said he had never in his life read such a letter and attempted to read it aloud. As he stood there red-faced and visibly shaken, tears began to show in his eyes. The letter had disturbed him so much that he was on the verge of crying and couldn't speak. He handed the letter to the Sister, and nodded at her to read it. She read the letter out loud and came upon a part that mentioned the priest was "a devil and a liar." After she finished, the Sister told us to stand up and say a prayer for the very bad girl who wrote the nasty letter.

Neither the father nor the Sister told us why he was being called a devil and a liar. There had to be a reason; just like our parents taught us — there was a reason for everything. I never found out how he got ahold of that letter, or who had written it, but I suppose we were to believe the girl had committed a sin by calling the priest a devil and a liar.

When I was growing up, the local Dene people still had very strong traditional values and spiritual beliefs. So it was not unusual for some of them to make offerings to nature. To the Dene people, such offerings were done out of respect and were more as a form of appeasement to nature rather than they were a religious act. However, such offerings were regarded as paganistic and ritualistic in the eyes of the priests and Sisters. They did not understand, nor did they try to understand, that it was our way of life. They could have tried to include some of the common spiritual beliefs into their religious ceremonies. They could have introduced Jesus as a great medicine man, or compared the offering of a lamb, as stated in the Bible, to the Dene Fire Feeding ceremony. Instead, they came with the attitude that "my God is better than your God".

Had they made an effort to include common spiritual beliefs in their religious ceremonies, I'm sure we would have had a better understanding of Christianity, especially the Roman Catholic religion. Instead, the priests and Sisters regarded our offerings, rituals and other such ceremonies as sinful or witchcraft.

The early missionaries regarded the Dene people and other native peoples as, in their own words, "lost in the wilderness". I find this ironic, as they would have been the ones lost in the wilderness without the help of the Native peoples. I also think that the Dene people got baptized more out of novelty, or thinking it was the proper thing to do, rather than out of pure faith and belief.

I think there is some misunderstanding among a lot of people with regard to the difference between Native spirituality and religion. Native spirituality is based on oral tradition and stories handed down from generation to generation. These stories formed the basis of a moral code, such as respect for others, respect for nature, honesty, and so on. Our beliefs are based on stories that explain things like dreams and visions, medicine (power), and elements of nature, like lightning. Other stories explain the overall concept of creation. From these stories and traditions came our values, which we learn as we grow up, and also influence the way we treat the land, animals and other people. In my culture, the Dene people shared in this common knowledge of living and depended on each other as an important means of survival, especially in the north.

Religion, on the other hand, I think, is based on some doctrine or principle and written instructions. As such, it is an institutionalized belief system. It is an imported system brought in by the missionaries, based on their own culture. The lessons were based on the notion that what they were doing was for our own good. In the residential school, we had to learn to adapt to these beliefs.

I remember one summer day, the Father Superior — the same one who was called a devil and a liar — was making his rounds among the tents in the field behind the Hudson's Bay compound. He spoke to a few people he happened to meet, just the usual chitchat, nothing of importance.

Some of us kids stood by a tent and watched an Elderly Woman as she knelt by her fireplace and burned some small pieces of fur, which I think was lynx. She was doing this as a small offering, praying for her husband and some other men who had gone on a hunting trip. I suppose she was praying for good weather and for a successful hunt.

Just then, the Father Superior happened to walk by. Suddenly, he stopped, saw what was going on and rushed over to the elderly woman. He started to kick dirt onto the fire, saying it was a sin for her to be making her offerings. He quickly made several signs of the cross with his hands over the smoking fireplace, while he continued to kick dirt on it. The elderly woman just sat back on her heels, probably amazed and surprised by the priest's actions. I don't think she really knew how to react to the situation. We watched, unsure of what to do. Finally, we just walked away. I don't know what happened after that between the Father and the Elderly Woman. Such offerings, like our language, were forbidden.

There were also incidents that seemed to contradict our teachings about what was and was not sinful. I remember one summer, there were so many grasshoppers that there was a danger they might damage or even destroy the mission's potato crop, so the Brothers placed piles of dried and green grass in and around the potato fields. These grass piles attracted the grasshoppers in the evenings, and early in the mornings, the Brothers would set the grass piles on fire. The grasshoppers would take to the air in all directions, trying to avoid the fire. There were so many of them that at times they looked like miniature cloud formations just a few feet above the ground. The fire would burn some grasshoppers but not enough to kill them all.

The situation became serious enough that one day, the priest led a religious procession around the settlement, reciting the Liturgy of the Saints in Latin to get rid of the grasshoppers. I wondered, wasn't this ritualistic or even pagan-like? Wasn't it also pagan and ritualistic when the priest burned incense, or prayed before a statue?

When I returned home for the summer from the residential school, some of the people in the various camps continued to make offerings, but these were always done in secrecy. Over time, it was seldom done and eventually the practice stopped. But I am glad that today, these ceremonies and drum dances are happening again in the communities at tribal assemblies and special events.

Back home, the early fall was usually the time of the year when the fish were running, so it was time to stock up on whitefish for the oncoming winter. It got a little bit cold to be out on the river checking nets at this time of the year. A few hardy people still made the journey into the settlement for supplies, but before long, the river ice made it impossible to travel in the canvas-covered canoes.

At the residential school, the mission also stocked up on whitefish. The Brothers and some hired men from the settlement had gone to fish near the area where the Kakisa River empties into Beaver Lake. They made several trips back to the mission in the scows loaded with whitefish. Whenever they returned with a load of fish, it was usually time for us to get to work.

Our job was to haul the fish from the scows up the riverbank to an enclosed compound below a ravine by the priests' residence. It was difficult, at times, to take the fish out of the scows because eggs would seep out of the fish and cover the floor, creating a slippery and slimy mess. The Brothers would then splash a pail of water into the scows to clean them up a bit.

Sometimes on our way up the riverbank, we would bump into other boys, often dropping the fish. When this happened, we all yelled, "Hey, watch it!" or "Watch where you're going!" No one said, "I'm sorry" or "Excuse me."

Once, a couple of years later, I was in the classroom and had sat behind a girl who wore a long ponytail. Every now and then, I would tug on her ponytail. Suddenly, she turned around and said loudly, "Stop it!" The teacher told me to leave and stand by the classroom door. Then he came out and told me to apologize to the girl. I didn't know what 'apologize' meant and I was afraid to ask.

My cousin, Margaret, was working in the kitchen with some other girls and heard what was going on. She walked by me on her way to the priests' dining room and whispered to me, "Say, 'I'm sorry'".

I thought that you said sorry only when someone had died, or you said you were sorry to God because you had committed a sin. I was confused and didn't know what to think. The teacher asked me one more time to apologize to the girl. After some hesitation, I walked back into the classroom and said to her, "I'm sorry."

After this episode, the Sister in one of the classes taught us manners and proper etiquette. I suspect that the teacher had talked to the Sisters about what had happened in his classroom. At least something good resulted from this episode.

The enclosed compound was fairly large with high, rough, wooden walls. It resembled a fort, except no one was attacking this one, only a few brave ravens and whiskey jacks on feeding raids. Inside the compound, other boys were helping a Brother hang the fish on wooden rafters. The fish were hung four or five high, and a stick held about eight to ten fish, skewered through the tail section. It took two of us to carry the fish, two sticks at a time, up the riverbank and to the compound. Some of the boys used wheelbarrows, which made it easier to carry more sticks of fish.

Sometimes when we had fish for supper, one of the boys would say, "Hey, I think this is the fish I brought up to the compound." Then someone else would say, "I recognize this fish. I carried it by its fins." Then the other boys would join in with their own claims on the fish and it would get noisy. It was a lot of fun, until the Sister demanded silence.

Hauling all the fish up the riverbank to the compound took the better part of the day. Once all the hauling and hanging was completed, the older boys helped the Brothers cover the top of the compound with branches and pieces of lumber to keep out the ravens and whiskey jacks. All that hung fish would serve as part of our food for the winter at the residential school, including food for the mission dog team.

CHAPTER SIX

My mom and dad came to visit Josie and me a couple of times during the months before Christmas. They brought us candies and sometimes they would bring dried moose meat; this certainly was a big treat for us. We didn't get traditional food, like dried meat or dried fish, at the residential school.

My parents would ask how we were doing and if everything was okay. We usually said we were fine so they wouldn't have to worry about us. They would tell us bits of news about my grandparents and the other people in Lishamie, staying about half an hour or so, or until one of the Sisters came and got us.

On one of these visits, my dad told us that my mother would be going far away. Apparently, the X-rays the doctor had taken of her at last summer's treaty time had come back positive, confirming that she had tuberculosis. The diagnosis meant she would have to go to the hospital in another community. My dad said she was scheduled to leave on the next available plane, possibly to Fort Rae or Fort Simpson. He said he didn't know how long she would be gone from home, but that one thing was certain: if my mom stayed away until she was cured, it would be for a very long, long time.

We sat next to my mother as she held our hands, speaking to us almost in a whisper. She told us to behave, listen to the Sisters, and try not to get into any trouble. She said she would write to us if she found someone who spoke Slavey and was able to write the letter in English for her.

A short while later, one of the Sisters came into the parlour area, indicating that the visit was over. I remember my mother hugged and kissed us. Then the Sister came over and led us away. I looked back at my mother. She was standing next to my dad, smiling and watching us.

I didn't know it then, but this was to be the last time I would ever see my mother. I always picture her standing there, smiling, and all of us not realizing it was to be our last time together as a whole family.

&

Life at the residential school was becoming routine, the same thing most every day. I was getting used to it now, although at times I did miss my parents and grandparents very much. I was alright during the daytime when I was in school or playing in the yard with the other kids. This kept my mind off thinking about home. But sometimes at night, I began to think about my parents and home. At such times I would get emotional and feel really homesick; sometimes I would put my head under the blankets and cry softly. I didn't want the other boys to hear me, and I especially did not want the Sisters to hear me, for fear they would think I was crying for nothing. I think most of us just accepted the fact that there was really nothing much we could do to change our situation.

At that time, there must have been at least thirty to forty boys in the residential school and probably the same number of girls. As it is typical in such numbers, kids do tease each other. Sometimes we would hear a boy yelling, *"Ma Soeur, Ma Soeur!"* which means "My Sister, My Sister!" in English. He would be trying to get the Sister's attention for help. Sometimes the Sister would respond by demanding to know what was going on, to which the boy's reply was usually something like, "He called my name," meaning, "He called me names!" In most cases, the Sister didn't really settle anything between the boys and the incident was forgotten. It all seemed to depend on the mood of the Sister at that particular moment. If the situation annoyed her, she would scold the offenders.

The Sisters spoke mainly in French, with some broken English mixed in, so this is what we heard and learned during our first year at the residential school. I remember one of the Sisters would get annoyed whenever things were scattered around the recreation area. She would make us clean up, pointing at the mess and saying, "Same chicken house, same chicken house." Her English was pretty bad, to say the least. What she probably meant was that our recreation area was as messy as the chicken coop, but we got the message.

Late one Saturday afternoon, the Sister called us into the building for supper. We came in, took off our jackets and sat at our places on the benches in the recreation area. Then she told some of the older boys that they were to remain after supper to help set up the benches in the dinning area for a movie. I'd never seen a movie in my life, but I'd heard some of the other kids talk about the movies they had seen. This was going to be a new experience for me.

At supper that evening, like the other kids, I was getting excited thinking about the movie and what it was going to be all about. The talk around the table that evening was about movies that some of the other kids had seen the past summer at a movie house in Fort Simpson. When I think about it now, their interpretation of what they saw or understood of the movies was pretty funny, and probably exaggerated.

After supper, the older boys placed the tables on top of each other against one of the walls. The benches were placed in neat rows: one section for the boys and another for the girls. A table was placed in the middle of the floor just behind the rows of benches. Finally, a large, white sheet was hung from the ceiling near the front wall. This was to be the movie screen.

Once everything was set up, the older boys returned to the recreation room. There, the Sister walked to the centre of the room, reached into her pocket and pulled out her little black notebook. She read out a few names and asked these boys she had just named to stand up. Then she told them that they were to go upstairs to bed; they would not see the movie. Apparently, some of them had behaved badly and now they were being punished for it. These boys got in a single file and were all sent upstairs to bed. Some of them cried because they didn't understand why they were being punished. I wondered what the boys had done that was bad behaviour. The Sister didn't give any reasons; she had their names in her little notebook and to her, that was what mattered. The rest of us went back to the dining area and settled on the benches opposite the girls and waited.

After awhile, one of the Brothers arrived with what looked like two suitcases containing the projector and the speaker. He placed the projector on the table next to a metal canister, which held the films, then he carried the speaker up the aisle between the benches and placed it on a table behind the large, white sheet that was hanging there. Pulling a wire out of the speaker box, he asked some of the boys to string it back to the projector.

When everything was ready, the Sisters called for silence as the Brother turned on the projector. The majority of the films were from the National Film Board: programs like Eyewitness News, and documentary-style films about some cowboys rounding up wild horses. There was also a short film about a day in the life of two members of a young women's choir either in Montreal or Toronto.

This was totally not what I had expected. Whatever happened to the cowboys and Indians that I had heard so much about at suppertime? I sat and watched, however, a little amazed at my first movie experience, wondering how the people in the movie were talking or singing and how we could actually see other people and cars moving behind them in some scenes.

Later, we were able to watch other films that came to the residential school, such as musicals. We would watch these over and over again. It was not because we liked them so much, but because the Sisters wanted us to learn some of the songs. These included *Auld Lang Syne, Waltzing Matilda,* a song about Barbara Ellen, and various other novelty songs. We learned these songs and sometimes sang them for the priests and Brothers at special occasions. We gave performances for the Bishop, Mother Provincial, Father Provincial, and any other church dignitary, whenever they visited the residential school. We also performed for Father Superior and Sister Superior on their birthdays or in honour of the feast of their patron saints. We were probably the only source of entertainment around at the residential school. Although my first experience with movies wasn't with the action-type movies of today, it did satisfy my curiosity.

One day, the Sister announced that we were all going for a picnic. There was some excitement, as we would be leaving the confines of the residential schoolyard and going out into the bush.

Some of the older boys had bows and arrows, which they brought with them from home or had made at the residential school. The bows were either made out of willow, spruce or birch. The arrows were made from straight pieces of willow, about sixteen to eighteen inches in length, and some of the arrows had two or three feathers tied to one end with sinew or thread. Most of the arrowheads were made of empty 30-30 caliber shell casings, flattened and filed to a sharp point. Some of the boys were skilled enough to kill small game with these arrows, such as prairie chicken, spruce grouse, rabbits and squirrels. Other boys had slingshots made from strips of inner tubes from truck tires.

Sometimes, the boys would bring in their kills to the residential school kitchen, and, depending on the cook, would even get to enjoy it at mealtime that evening or the following day.

Going on these picnics would be a happy occasion for all of us because we were able to run around free in the bush without restrictions, even if it only lasted for a little while. We were born on the land, and the bush was our familiar environment, so we enjoyed every bit of these brief stints of freedom.

On these outings some of us, especially the younger ones, were not allowed to speak our own language. We were constantly reminded that God was everywhere, hearing and seeing everything, even when we were out playing in the fields or playing hide and seek in the bushes. So when we were in the bush playing, we used to whisper when we spoke to each other in our own language. After awhile, we'd throw caution to the wind and talk loudly to each other, not really caring who was listening out there. But every now and then we'd look up, just in case.

The bush was our familiar environment as we were born on the land. We knew few English words for some of the trees and plants, but we knew their names in our language. We enjoyed every bit of this brief stint of freedom.

About one kilometre from the residential school was a log cabin that everyone referred to as the "Boys' Shack." The girls also had a similar log cabin. The "Girls' Shack" was about the same distance from the residential school, but it was located further towards the banks of the Snye. I suppose this was the mission's attempt to present some semblance of our traditional way of life. But what it lacked was traditional food.

I don't remember too much of what we ate on these outings. Perhaps it wasn't that great because it didn't leave a lasting impression on my mind. There were no hot-dogs or hamburgers back then, at least not in Fort Providence. These kinds of food came much later in my life. But I do remember the Sisters making pancakes. They would mix some flour and water in a large enamel bowl, then pour the thin mixture one ladle-full at a time on top of the hot stove.

In the winter, when we were at the Boys' Shack, the Sisters sometimes made a kind of taffy out of sugar and syrup, boiling the mixture with some water. Once most of the water had boiled away, they would take the pail outside. Then they would pour the brownish sweet mixture onto the snow in small lumps. We'd curl the syrupy candy at the end of a stick while it was still warm and make something like a Popsicle. One of the Sisters said that making this kind of candy reminded her of her parents' home back in Quebec where they did the same thing with maple syrup, especially in the springtime.

When we were not playing in the bush, the Sisters would gather us in the shack or outside by the door for a sing-a-long. We used to sing mostly French-Canadian folk songs, like the fishermen songs we had heard and watched in the National Film Board movies. Maybe the Sisters were homesick too, and they sang them with us under the pretext of teaching us some of the songs. To this day, I still remember many of these songs and can still sing at least a line or two from some of them.

When we were at the Boys' Shack, we'd play hide and seek or other games in the bushes. Sometimes, we had improvised archery contests. One boy would place a piece of board or a can on a tree stump, count so many steps back and make a mark on the ground. The boys with bows and arrows would then try to knock the target off the tree stump. Some of us younger boys would retrieve the arrows for the older boys, and they would try all over again.

We were never allowed to go near the Girls' Shack or anywhere in the vicinity. This area was "no man's land." One day, we were on our way back to the residential school after one of these picnics when we saw some girls across the field on the bank of the ravine near the Girls' Shack. One of the boys let out a loud whistle at the girls. Immediately, the Sister told him that he had done a very bad thing because whistling was like calling for the devil. She told us it was evil to be whistling at girls. Perhaps, instead, she should have told us that it wasn't polite to whistle at people, but we were not taught proper manners. The mention of sin always discouraged any kind of potentially perceived evil or sinful action.

When we were out hunting in the bush, we often whistled at rabbits and small game birds. Our whistling usually made the rabbit stop running and the birds land. What would we do now that we couldn't whistle while hunting? What would happen if we did whistle? Would the devil appear? Such rules, which actually bordered on mental abuse, really created confusion in our young minds and lives.

꙰

The snow had long ago covered the ground and it was my first winter at the residential school. There was some talk among the boys about Christmas. The priest had mentioned the birth of Jesus on Christmas Day during catechism classes. Some of the Sisters had already begun decorating the chapel at the residential school. I didn't pay too much attention to this; I just thought it was a regular routine of the residential school.

One day in the classroom, the Sister told us that we could draw Christmas cards for whomever we wanted. As it was my first experience with this, I didn't know anything about Christmas cards or their significance. So before I did anything, I watched the other boys as they drew winter scenery with crayons onto pieces of paper. Some drew a picture of a church, a big Christmas tree, a manger or just a plain, big star on the paper.

We drew things and scenes that, to us, depicted Christmas as it had been taught to us or as we understood it back then. One of the boys drew a picture of a dog team. I suppose the boy was trying to show his parents coming into the settlement for Christmas and their only means of transportation was by dog team, but the Sister told him it was not really a Christmas scene. We made the cards mostly for the priests, Brothers and Sisters, because we thought it was the thing to do, and scribbled

Merry Christmas in English or French on the front or back.

We were at our desks drawing the cards when one of the boys suggested that maybe we could make cards for our parents. We all thought it was a good idea but we were afraid to ask the Sister. We just looked at each other and waited to see who would do it. Finally, one of the boys walked over to the Sister and asked her if we could make cards for our parents. To our surprise, she also thought it was a good idea.

At that time, my dad was home alone with one of my brothers and my mom was away at some hospital. I wasn't sure if I should make two cards: one for my dad and the other for my mom, but I didn't know where to send the card for my mom so I decided to make one card for the both of them.

I didn't know what to draw for my parents because they already knew about winter scenery. I decided to draw something religious on one side of the card, so I drew a star in one corner and as best I could, drew an angel in the other corner. Then I drew lines representing light from the star shining on the angel. Actually, I did the religious scene to please the Sister more than anything else. On the other side of the card I drew a Christmas tree with bright yellow lights here and there. Finally, I wrote Joyeux Noel on the front and Merry Christmas on the back of the card.

The colouring on the card was pretty crude because we only had crayons to use back then. I mixed some of the colours and rubbed my picture lightly with the tips of my fingers and it didn't look too bad. I wasn't quite sure how the card would be sent to my dad, who was either in the bush on his trapline or at Lishamie. So I just wrote his name on the homemade envelope and gave it to the Sister.

The Sisters had us participate in all kinds of practices in

preparation for the Christmas concert. We practiced songs in English and French. We also practiced role-playing for the Nativity scene, with some of us dressed up as cows or sheep lying on the grass in front of the manger. A couple of the boys had white sheets draped over them, with a narrow strip of cloth tied around their heads. They were supposed to be shepherds. The choir members, all girls, practiced various hymns and other religious Christmas songs.

Christmas that first year at the residential school was a new experience for me. We never had Christmas at our village; at least, I don't recall a decorated Christmas tree, toys, or anything else that resembled Christmas. Some of the boys who had been through this event told us about going to the big church at midnight, and that there was also a man in a red suit with a long, white beard who gave out toys and candies. They also talked about having corn flakes for breakfast on Christmas morning, food I don't ever remember having back home.

The real happy news was that we would be permitted to visit our parents for the day. This meant leaving the confines of the residential school and going out into the settlement. As Christmas Day approached, we would see various families arriving by dog teams as they went by the residential school on the other side of the fence. Some families came from as far away as Redknife River and Kakisa Lake. Some of the dog teams had harnesses decorated with ribbons and tassels made of yarn. Some of the dogs had wide, decorated straps on their backs that were embroidered with yarn. We would watch from the windows to see if we could recognize anyone going by.

The evening before Christmas, we all went to bed earlier than usual. At about 10:30, the Sister began waking us up.

We all got out of bed, washed up, and dressed up in white

shirts and special jackets that the Sister had given us to wear for the midnight mass. Then we all filed downstairs to the recreation area, where the Sister gave each of us a cup of very thin porridge mixed with milk. We were not allowed to eat solid food because we would be going to communion, so this was like a very light snack. The midnight mass was going to last for about two hours or so.

While we sat and sipped on the thin porridge mixture, the Sister went around with her notebook to let some of the boys know how much money they had left. Back then, we used to ask the Sister, "How much money do I have left in my name?" We never used the word 'account,' nor did we know of such a word. The Sister asked if the boys would donate to the collection during the midnight mass. Naturally, all the boys agreed. You never said no to a priest or to a Sister. Before going out to the church, the Sister gave the boys their money, all of it in coins.

Soon, in single file we went downstairs and out into the chilly night on our way to the big church. As we crossed the girls' yard, we could see some dog teams tied up to the fence that ran between the church and the residential school. We could also hear a few bells jingle from the dogs' harnesses.

The church was packed as we entered and went to our assigned pews. I saw my dad briefly in the crowd as we came in but I couldn't run over and hug him. Still, I was really happy to see that he was there, but I didn't show that emotion on the outside. By now, I had learned how to hide my emotions, so I just kept that happy feeling inside to myself.

The church was decorated with a nativity scene on the left side close to the altar. There were small statues of the baby Jesus, the Virgin Mary, Saint Joseph and a number of other statues of shepherds and animals, all which had been put in proper places. Several small spruce trees were placed around the nativity scene.

The midnight service consisted of three masses, so it lasted until well after two in the morning. One of the Brothers passed a collection basket around. People put dollar bills and coins into the basket. Some of the boys dropped their coins into the basket. This was my first experience with the collection. I didn't know what it was all about or who took the money.

At last, the midnight mass was over. We all waited as the people from the settlement made their way out of the church through the main door. Then we waited again for the girls as they walked out the side door. Finally, it was our turn to make our way out of the church. We walked out into the chilly air again and back to our recreation area. Then we all climbed upstairs to the dormitory to sleep for a few hours before the usual wake-up time.

Although at my first Christmas at the residential school, the man with the long beard in a red suit didn't show up, there were plenty of toys and candies. There was a big Christmas tree in the middle of the dining area. Underneath the tree were many wrapped toys in all shapes, sizes and colours. The Sisters called out our names and one by one, we went up to get our present. There were glass trains, plastic fire trucks, spinning toys, plastic soldiers, toy guns, plastic cars, trucks, and so on. A lot of these things I had never seen before and they had no relation whatsoever to the lifestyle I had known and been used to. These were definitely changing times for me.

I remember we got corn flakes, milk and toast for breakfast that Christmas morning. I also remember that we sang grace before and after breakfast. On Boxing Day morning, we got up with excitement and anticipation, as some of us would be allowed to visit our parents for the whole day. Some of the boys whose parents lived too far away, in places like Jean Marie River or Fort Simpson, didn't get this privilege. Some of them cried at this time of the year. It was a sad time for them, as some of them hadn't been home for years.

My dad came for Josie and me that morning, shortly after breakfast. It sure was nice to see him again and I was happy that we would be staying with him for the whole day. As we left the building, he told us that he was staying with my Uncle Louis and his family. He would be going back to Lishamie within the next few days. Our grandparents had returned to Lishamie on Christmas Day. Maybe we would get to see them when they came back to the settlement for Easter. My dad told us that he hadn't heard from my mother yet, adding that maybe she couldn't find anyone to write a letter for her. He never said anything about the Christmas card that I made for him and I didn't say anything about it, either.

For the better part of the day, like most of the other kids, we drove the dog team all over the settlement. Dog teams were like Ski-Doos for us back then. We only came into the house to warm up or have something to eat, and then we were out again. Poor dogs, they had to pull us around all day. I bet they were happy to see us go back to the residential school so they could rest up.

All too soon, the day was over and we had to return to the residential school. My dad walked us back, reluctantly I think, because instead of the usual shortcut across the field behind the Hudson's Bay compound, we went the long way around. We walked to the riverbank and followed the main road to the grey building. The Sisters were in the parlour waiting for us and the other kids. My father told us he would visit again before Easter and left.

CHAPTER SEVEN

After the Christmas excitement finally died down, life returned to the usual routine at the residential school. It was sometime after the New Year that I heard the news about my mother. I was playing outside with the other boys when one of the Sisters called me in. There was always some nervous anticipation whenever the Sister called you in. You never knew the reason until the last minute, when she decided to tell you. I came into the building, went upstairs to the recreation area and took off my parka. The Sister came over and told me to go to the chapel right away because my mother had passed away.

I stood there and didn't know what to think or say. It was so sudden, and the Sister's voice was sharp, like a command, telling me to go to the chapel immediately. There was no sensitivity in the tone of her voice. Shocked, I just nodded my head and walked slowly down the hallway towards the chapel. I didn't know what to expect. Maybe my mother would be there; I was a little scared.

There was no one in the chapel. It was silent, except for the slight echo of my footsteps and the sound of me clearing my throat. I still didn't know what to expect or what to do, so I knelt in the second or third pew by the entrance. After some time, I heard footsteps coming down the hallway. The chapel door opened and I saw one of the Sisters look inside. When she saw me, she came in and walked over to where I was kneeling. It was Sister Kristoff, who knew my parents. In a whispered voice, she asked what I was doing in the chapel. I told her that my mother had passed away and that I had been told to go to the chapel.

As she knelt down beside me, she whispered, "We will say some Hail Mary's for her", and we said the prayers together. Then she stood up and sat next to me on the pew. Gently, she put her arm around me and held me. I looked up at her and saw tears in her eyes and I began to cry. It was the first and only time that a nun had shown any kind of sympathy to me.

I was seven years old and did not quite understand the full meaning of losing a parent, but that Sister's kindness left a lasting impression on me and I never forgot her for it. The nuns I knew never showed very much emotion. But Sister Kristoff was the exception; she showed compassion for me and gave me some comfort at a time when I really needed it. After I left the residential school, I made it a point to see her at the Sisters' residence whenever I was in Fort Providence.

I cried as she held me and whispered that my mother was in heaven and would be looking after me from then on. No one else came around to see how I was doing in the chapel, so she stayed with me for awhile. Later, she walked me back to the boys' recreation room and asked me to go to mass the next day and pray for my mother.

I barely slept that night. I stayed awake, trying to remember what my mother looked like. I tried to remember some of the things we did and the happy moments we had when I was home with her and my dad. I remembered her crying when she heard the news about my little brother.

I remembered her saying, "My poor little boy went away all alone among strangers." Now it was her turn to go away far from home and among strangers.

My final image of my mother was at her last visit with us sometime before Christmas. She was standing next to my dad, smiling and watching us as we left the visiting area. It seemed so long ago. I was seven years old and now without a mother. I cried again and tried to sleep.

Years later, I visited Sister Kristoff at the Grey Nuns retirement home in Edmonton. I introduced her to my wife, Esther, my five-year-old son, Rory-Jon and my two-year-old daughter, Tara. She was happy to see me and any other northern visitors, especially those from Fort Providence. She would put her hands in my coat pockets and say, "Take my love and prayers back to Fort Providence with you."

Then one day I was informed that Sister Kristoff had passed away. I think she was then in her late eighties. I always thought of her as the only nun who had a true calling for her vocation. I believe some became nuns because it had been a family tradition, not necessarily because of any religious commitment or conviction. Maybe this is what caused the Sisters to take their frustrations out on the children in the form of physical and mental abuse. I am not trying to make excuses for them or for their actions. I just feel there has to be some reason or explanation behind such cruel behaviour, and this is the only logical reason I can think of.

It was sometime later that my dad came to visit us. The news of my mother passing away had long reached him and he was aware that we already knew. He didn't say too much; he spoke mostly about how our grandparents were doing. Sister Kristoff came over and offered her condolences.

When our visit was over, my dad gave us some change he had in his pocket and said he would most likely be back at Easter before leaving for the spring hunt.

Sometimes during visits, parents gave money to their kids. The kids gave the money to the Sister, and she had a little notebook where she kept a record of the money. Whenever we bought anything, she would deduct the amount and tell us how much money we had left. Sometimes, we were allowed to go to the mission store to buy candies. Other times, we'd go to the storage room above the chapel, where we bought not only candies, but also some religious pictures, medallions or rosaries. I don't remember ever going to the Hudson's Bay store during my stay at the residential school.

Occasionally, the Sister would call us in and ask if any of us wanted to make a donation for a special mass to be celebrated for the Pope, the Bishop or for some other religious occasion. Other times, she would ask if any of us wanted to buy a rosary or a medallion that had been blessed by the priest, or a small religious picture, which we could put in our hymn book or missal. At times like this, no one refused her request.

A week or so after New Year's, the Sisters told us about another special religious celebration called "Epiphany"—a celebration to commemorate the three wise men, who came to Jesus on the eve of his birth. I didn't understand the significance of this religious event; it was simply yet another occasion to go to church.

After attending mass, we changed back into our one-piece

denim coveralls and marched downstairs to the dining area for lunch: as always, boys on one side of the room and girls on the other. After our plates were cleared away, one of the Sisters announced there was a surprise for us.

"Now, there are cupcakes for all of you," she said, passing them out to us. "But be careful not to bite too hard. One boy and one girl will find a marble inside their cupcakes, and these two lucky children will be crowned king and queen for the day."

There were some giggles and anticipation as we all proceeded to eat our cupcakes, being careful not to bite into the marble. We glanced around to search out the boy and girl who would be granted royal status. Commotion among the boys and girls revealed the winners, and the Sisters asked the pair to come forward to the centre of the dining room.

The two seemed apprehensive and a little embarrassed as the Sister placed capes around their shoulders and crowns upon their heads. The Sisters smiled and seemed to be amused by the whole thing, clapping their hands to congratulate the king and queen. The whole coronation seemed silly, and once it was over, the "king" joined the boys and the "queen" joined the girls and we went on with the rest of our day.

The Sisters, however, continued the game at supper that evening. In the centre of the dining room was a small table covered with a white cloth. The Sisters had prepared this special table for the king and queen, who, with crowns once again placed on their heads, sat quietly and ate their meals without looking around. We all could see that they both desperately wanted the whole thing to end as soon as possible.

After supper, and without any further ceremony, the king

FROM LISHAMIE

and queen lost their capes and crowns and regained their status as regular people. This was the closest thing to a date that the Sisters allowed to happen. I think the whole event was staged more for the amusement of the Sisters than anything else.

In catechism classes, we learned that Easter was the day to commemorate Jesus' rise from the dead. The priest called this the resurrection of Jesus. We also learned that the few weeks before Easter was called the period of Lent. According to the Roman Catholic religion, it was to be a time of prayer, sacrifice and fasting. This was a forty-day period, which I think started on Ash Wednesday and continued to Easter Sunday. The priest told us that to give up something during Lent was a form of sacrifice. Some of us decided to give up something during Lent, or at least try to give up something, like eating candy, which there was very little of, anyway, or skipping a meal or eating less of something at mealtime, which some of us gladly did.

Some of the boys attempted to attend mass every day during the whole forty days of Lent. Some of the stubborn ones succeeded. There was no physical reward awaiting anyone completing a sacrifice or a fasting period. We were told that we would get some spiritual reward. We went to school and did our chores as usual during the weeks leading up to Easter. In the classroom, we made cards wishing everyone Happy Easter. Everything was similar to the school activities at Christmas time. This was going to be my first Easter at the residential school. I don't remember celebrating Easter at home, so this was going to be something new for me.

Easter in the South Slavey language translates to mean "the day the sun dances." Some say that if you look at the sun, you can see the sun's rays in the form of a cross and that you can actually see the cross move up and down. Out of curiosity,

102

I tried looking into the sun briefly, but I didn't see anything. It only hurt my eyes. The only thing I could see after that was a bunch of blue and black dots for the next hour or so. I never did look directly at the sun again. My curiosity was satisfied.

There were several religious services during the week leading up to Easter Sunday. It started with the prayers on Thursday evening. Then there was the "Way of the Cross" service that took place on Friday evening. At this service, the priest covered all of the statues and crucifixes in the chapel with pieces of black cloth to signify the death of Christ and the darkness that covered the world. Anything representing some kind of joy or happiness was not allowed.

On Easter Sunday morning, we all went to mass in the chapel. During the service, the priest took the black cloths off all the statues and crucifixes. Candles were lit around the altar and in various places throughout the chapel, signifying the risen Christ symbolically bringing light back into the world. Bells were rung at appropriate times during the services, also signifying joy and happiness again in the world.

After the morning service, we all went back to our recreation area. Shortly thereafter, we went downstairs for breakfast. We went to our usual places at the table and saw corn flakes in all the bowls. After the Sister said grace, we sat down to eat. Then the Sister passed around some toast. This was just like breakfast on Christmas morning.

After breakfast, we did our chores and played for awhile. Then we all got ready for the High Mass to be held in the big church. This was just like any other Sunday, except today was Easter Sunday. We dressed up like we had done for Christmas midnight mass. The Sister gave us all white shirts and gave neckties to some of the boys. We also wore the special jackets.

Then, as usual, we got into single file and marched out into the chilly air to the big church.

The church was crowded with people, just like it had been at Christmas time. A lot of them came in from the outlying villages and camps. For some, it would be their last trip into the settlement until the ice left the river. The Easter Sunday mass was a little longer than the regular Sunday mass but much shorter than the midnight mass. When the mass was over, we returned to our recreation area, changed into our coveralls again and gave back the special jackets to the Sister, who put them away in a box for another special occasion.

Later that day, the Sister told us that we would be able to spend the next day in the settlement with our parents if they came for us. This was going to be just like Christmas, when we spent the day with my dad.

Sometime during the morning of Easter Monday, my dad came for my sister and me. It sure was nice to be out of the fenced-in yard of the residential school. This was freedom for the day! My grandparents weren't in the settlement for Easter so we didn't get to see them. We stayed at my Uncle Louis' place. My aunt had some dried moose meat, so we ate our fill of this. We spent the rest of the day visiting with some friends and relatives who were in the settlement and travelled around with the dog team.

Sometime in the early evening, my dad called us into the house. Visiting day was over and it was time for us to return to the residential school. The day seemed too short, especially because I knew that the next day, life at the residential school would return to the usual routine.

I turned eight years old in June during my first year at the residential school. A Sister had told me it was my birthday; I didn't get a present, nor did the boys around me sing "Happy Birthday." I was simply told that I was now eight years old. Along with some other boys, I went to special religious classes for a few days in preparation for confirmation. I didn't quite understand what this was all about and I'm sure the other boys were just as confused as I was.

I was confirmed along with other boys when the Bishop arrived at Fort Providence, on his way to visit other communities. Once again, the Sister took out the black blazers and the banners with gold-coloured tassels. We wore these as we had done for our first communion, and the girls also wore the white dresses and veils over their heads again.

During the confirmation service, the priest motioned to us to come forward. In single file, we went up and knelt at the railing by the altar. The Bishop gave his blessing to each of us and said something like, "Receive the Holy Spirit," then tapped each of us lightly on the cheek. Thereafter, we were considered as having received the rite of confirmation. Shortly after my confirmation, I began serving as an altar boy at some of the early morning masses. At that time, the mass was still conducted in Latin, so the altar boy's responses to the priest were also in Latin. For example, the priest would say, *"Dominus vobis cum,"* to which I would say, *"Et cum spirituum."*

Eventually, I memorized the required prayers and learned enough to serve as an altar boy during regular mass. After about two years, I graduated to serving at High Mass on Sundays and on other special occasions. By my third year at the residential school, I was able to read French, and I began to read the Latin in the Missal just like it was French. So although I never understood a word of Latin, I read and memorized the altar boy's responses in this way.

The priest also recited some of the prayers in Slavey, with a lot of mispronounced words. Most of the prayers had been translated from French to South Slavey. The French missionaries had used the modern alphabet to write down the words but they did not fully capture the sounds of the South Slavey language. As a consequence, some words and phrases used in various prayers didn't make too much sense. The prayers sound silly now when I remember, but the priests who had learned to speak the South Slavey language translated them, so we also learned these South Slavey prayers, mispronunciations and all.

One spring day in June, after all the snow had melted, the Sisters told us that there would be a field day for all the boys and girls. It was to be held at the local airstrip on Saint Jean-Baptiste Day. The activities would include races and other sports competition, and there would be prizes for the winners. Then the Sister told us that Saint Jean-Baptiste was the patron saint of all French Canadians. On Saint Jean-Baptiste Day, there were parades, concerts and other celebrations all over Quebec. This was a special day for the priests, Brothers and Sisters in Fort Providence and in other communities, as most of them came from Quebec.

In preparation for the day, the Sister told us to practice running, doing long jumps and other activities. Hearing this, everyone started running around and doing long jumps all over the place; it looked really disorganized. What the Sister had probably meant was that we should start exercising on a daily basis to get in shape for the upcoming field activities. A few of us did honestly try to exercise, but like any other kids, we found there were always other interesting forms of distractions.

School was coming to a close, but I wasn't aware, nor was I told, that some of us would be going home for the summer by the end of the June. Very few of us knew this.

Saint. Jean-Baptiste Day arrived, and as usual, we all went to church. After church, we had a quick lunch. Later, we went outside and watched one of the Brothers drive the old, red truck up to the kitchen area. Some of the boys helped the Brother load up the truck with food and other goodies, then, the Brother drove off with some of the boys riding in the back of the truck. Some of us ran alongside the truck for as long as possible until it finally out-distanced us.

The Sister called the rest of us together and we began to walk with her to the airstrip a couple of miles away. Back then, we never took notice of the distances we had to walk to get someplace, or how long it took.

We walked along the riverbank, passing by the church, the Bay, some private homes, and the Signal Corps compound. Sometimes when we walked by the Signal Corps compound and the door of the building was opened, we could hear the beep-beep of the Morse code signals. The signal was fairly loud, and I think they kept it loud because of the noise from the power generator. We did learn some Morse code in the Boy Scouts, but not enough to decipher the incoming messages.

After some time, we finally arrived at the end of the airstrip. It was covered with some gravel and patches of dried grass and foxtails. There were puddles of water here and there, remnants of the spring thaw. In the distance, we could see some of the boys running around and playing. We continued until we finally got to the area where the tables and boxes of food were, then some of us sat on the ground to rest up from the long walk.

A few hundred feet from the riverbank were a number of log cabins, connected with wooden sidewalks that were broken in some places. Small willow and raspberry bushes grew in between some of the cabins. These cabins and the broken sidewalks were the only visible remains of the presence of the American and Canadian armies, who had built the airstrip as part of a number of staging areas for the Norman Wells Canol project.

We walked around the log cabins; some still had their windows and doors boarded up. There was some commotion when someone found a couple of coins under the sidewalk. Then, one of the boys found a wristwatch. We all crowded around this boy, as some of us had never seen a wristwatch before. It was quite a novelty. Before long, everyone was looking under the sidewalks and searching around the cabins for something. We forgot about the races and prizes for a short time.

Finally, the Sister began blowing her whistle. Some of the boys put whatever they had found in their pockets as we ran over and gathered around her. She told us that the field day activities were about to get underway and that we should all get back to the truck on the airstrip.

The races were organized according to age groups. There was the usual straight line race, where you ran across the field, touched some object and ran back. We also had three-legged races, potato-sack races, wheel-barrow races, spoon races and many other games. I think the Sisters improvised some of these games on the spot. These were games we never played at home.

All the boys and girls took part in the races, but there were separate races for the boys and girls. We cheered each other on and laughed when someone fell or bumped into someone else, especially during the potato and spoon races. The winners got prizes, like candy, rosary and small religious pictures. After most of the races and other competitions were done, the Sisters called us together and we said grace. Then they gave us something to eat and drink.

After lunch, we were allowed to play for awhile before some of the activities resumed. Some of us went back to the army cabins and began looking for things again. One of the boys pulled the boards off a window, opened it and climbed into the cabin. He opened the door for us and we followed him in. Then someone else opened another cabin and some boys piled into that one, too.

We lost track of time again, as we were busy looking for things in and around the cabins. Then we heard the whistle blow as the Sister came briskly down the broken sidewalk, her arms swinging at her sides. We knew then that she wasn't coming over to help us look for things in the cabins. She stopped and yelled at us to get out of the cabins and bring her whatever we had found.

The boys brought her some coins, a couple of wristwatches, some paper matches and some other odds and ends, laying these offerings at the Sister's feet. There were even a couple of canned foods, like Prem or Spork. It must have been quite a comical sight. The Sister put all the stuff in a sack and gave it to the Father Superior, who promptly put it into the truck for safe-keeping.

Then, we were back on the field for some more races and other competitions. Later, we had some snacks and the Sisters passed out some more prizes to the winners. We said some prayers, and then it was time to go back to the residential school. Some of the Sisters and girls got into the back of the red truck, while the rest of us began the long walk back to the settlement and on to the residential school. We had all had an enjoyable day. It was a nice change from the fenced-in yard of the residential school.

On our way to a picnic and a field day on Saint Jean-Baptiste Day

CHAPTER EIGHT

A few days after the field day activities, the Sisters announced that some of us would be going home for the summer. There was great excitement when we learned that the local boys and girls would be going home by the coming weekend. Later that day, some of the boys brought boxes and suitcases into the recreation area. The Sister passed around the suitcases, calling out the names on the tags. From the boxes she took out some bags and passed them around to the rest of the boys to pack their personal belongings.

Finally, it dawned on me that I would be going home. I was actually leaving the residential school! Then I wondered who was going to let my dad know that we were going home. I prayed that somehow the news would get to him. For some of the boys and girls, there was no way for them to get home, so they would stay at the residential school over the summer months. Over the next couple of days, we talked about nothing else but going home and what we would do during the summer. Some of the boys said they would ask their parents not to send them back to the residential school in the fall.

Soon the day arrived for us to go home; there was anticipation and excitement in the air that morning, and some of us were so happy that we even got up early to go to mass. It would probably be the last mass we attended before returning in the fall. After breakfast, we began guessing as to who would be the first one to leave the residential school. A few of us looked out the windows and watched as some people began to arrive at the building. If we recognized someone's parents, we would call out to the boy and let him know that his mom or dad was coming for him. My dad came for my sister and me later that afternoon.

It was quite a feeling just to get out of the residential school, out of the fenced-in yard. I was leaving a place with rules that controlled my every move. It was like taking off an old jacket that you had on all winter and finally throwing it away. This was freedom! It was freedom to do what we liked without the force of discipline, at least for a couple of months. We stopped at the Bay as my dad bought a few things, then we walked down the riverbank to our canoe. One of my brothers was waiting there. We got into the canoe and paddled away to our village—Lishamie, occasionally stopping to let the canoe drift downstream with the current. We talked, laughed and pointed at familiar places along the shoreline.

Josie pointed to a place on the riverbank and mentioned that she remembered picking saskatoon berries with my mother. Immediately, I turned to look at my dad to see what would happen, a reaction probably due to my residential school conditioning. But the smile on my dad's face said it was all right to talk about my mother, even though she had passed away. He was probably glad, and also proud that we did not forget our mother.

Soon, we were at the mouth of the channel that ran by our village. We kept paddling and arrived at the houses, landing on a makeshift ramp of large spruce boughs and willow branches. Once we had pulled the canoe onto shore, my sister ran up the riverbank to my grandparents' house and I followed her. Grandmother hugged us and Grandfather looked at me and told me that I had grown a little. It sure was nice to be home again.

❧

No too much happened in the settlement of Fort Providence during the summer back when I was a young boy. Most everyone was living up or down the river at small permanent villages. It was much later on, sometime in 1960s, when the government began to build houses for some of the people. The first houses were built with local logs and eventually lumber was brought in for the construction of other houses.

I think the houses were used as incentives to entice people to move from their villages and into the settlement. This worked, because more houses were built and more people moved into the settlement from their camps. Eventually, all except two or three permanent villages were abandoned.

The big event during the summer was the arrival of the first freight barge at the settlement. The barge brought supplies for the Hudson's Bay Company, the RCMP, the Signal Corps, a local trader, and sometimes for the mission. The mission had its own boat and barge to haul material and supplies.

From the top of the riverbank, we were able to see any boat coming down the river. Then everyone would walk to the mission dock and watch as the boat docked the barges along the shore. A couple of deckhands jumped off the first barge and began tying up the rest of the barges to the shore. Some of the local young men had been hired to help unload the freight. Often, it took them all day and into the late evening to complete the unloading. The freight was either hauled away in the Signal Corps' truck or in the mission's old, red truck.

One day, after the freight was unloaded from the barges, eggs appeared on the shelves in the Hudson's Bay store. I think the eggs cost around ninety-five cents a dozen back then. We had eaten eggs before, but they had been duck, goose or seagull eggs that we'd gathered in early spring. We always boiled these eggs. But the store-bought eggs could be fried, and a panful of fried eggs sure tasted different than boiled eggs.

It was during that same summer that I had my first taste of an orange and an apple. The oranges and apples came individually wrapped in thin paper, and they were about ten cents each. For another ten cents, we could buy a chocolate bar or a package of gum. A bottle of pop was twenty-five cents. In South Slavey, a bottle of pop roughly translated means "something that cools you off." It was silly, though, because back then, there were no coolers in the store so we drank warm pop to cool off. All these new things were quite a novelty, and a sign of other changes that were eventually coming.

❧

In the Northwest Territories, Treaty 11 was signed with the Dene people in 1921, after oil was discovered at Norman Wells the previous year. I think this treaty, like many other treaties with First Nations across the country, was only a means of protecting the government's political and economic interests. Regardless, the event has been celebrated every summer since that time.

In mid-July, people began arriving at the settlement in anticipation of Treaty Day. The field behind the old Hudson's Bay compound would fill up with tents. The only private houses in the settlement belonged to a few Dene and Métis people, and a couple of white trappers. Everyone else lived in tents whenever they arrived and stayed in the settlement for no more than a couple of days.

The local RCMP strictly enforced prohibition during treaty gatherings. They would make their rounds unexpectedly, usually accompanied by one or two Signal Corps men. When they discovered a brew pot, they'd arrest the culprit and spill the brew right on the ground. I remember there was one zealous member of the RCMP who would shoot dogs with his revolver. He did this while driving among the tents in an open army jeep. Sometimes, you could hear a bullet ricochet off a rock, or hear the high-pitched sound as a bullet flew off in some direction. It was a wonder that no one got hit accidentally by a stray bullet. Thank goodness for poor marksmanship.

The Chief complained that it was dangerous and that there was a possibility a bullet might ricochet off a rock and accidentally hit someone, but the RCMP officer insisted that loose dogs had to be shot because they could have rabies. The officer told the people to be sure to tie up their dogs. Dogs were important to the people as a means of transportation in the winter, so everyone did their utmost to keep their dogs tied up. Some people even went as far as to leave their dogs loose on an island across from the settlement, returning to feed them every other day or so. The dogs were left there until the owners were ready to return to their villages or move to some other campsites.

The day before the government treaty party arrived, a large tent was erected in the field next to the fence of the Hudson's Bay compound. The next day, the treaty ceremony began with a customary meeting between Indian Affairs officials and the Chief and Council. The local RCMP officers were also present in their red uniforms. Periodically, there would be an election for the Chief or Councillors. This was done consensus style, with a show of hands from everyone present at the meeting who was old enough to vote. This was the accepted practice until Indian Affairs introduced election regulations some years later.

An Indian Affairs official would speak to the people first, followed by the Chief, and maybe the Councillors would say a few words. Once the opening ceremony was over, the Chief and some of his Councillors would sit next to the Indian Affairs officials and everyone would receive five dollars as treaty payment.

Back then, everyone had X-rays taken because of tuberculosis. A doctor was present and X-rays were taken in another special tent. There was a generator outside the tent that provided the necessary power for the X-ray machines.

During one Treaty Day, I became sick with a terrible headache. I threw up whatever I had eaten that morning. Finally, my dad brought me down to the doctor's boat, which was tied to the shore below the Hudson's Bay store. The doctor was fishing on the riverbank, and my dad explained my situation to him. The doctor motioned for us to follow him into the boat, where he examined me quickly and took my temperature. He gave me a couple of pills, which I took right away with a cup of water. Before we left, he told my dad that I was to wear a hat whenever I went outside because of the hot sun. By that evening, I was well enough again to play and run around with the other boys.

On the evening of Treaty Day, there was a feast by the Chief's tent. Everyone took part in the preparation and cooking of the food. Some of the young men would pass around flour, fish, moose meat and other food that was to be cooked. When everything was cooked, it was taken to the Chief's tent, and either he or one of his Councillors would fire a 30-30 rifle into the air to summon the people for the feast. Everyone brought their own plates, cups and utensils. Parents and children sat around long tablecloths and canvas that had been spread on the ground by the entrance to the Chief's tent.

Sometimes a member of the government treaty party would come to the feast and eat with the Chief and Council. The man usually came alone, dressed for the occasion in a suit and tie. He seemed rather out of place almost as if he was the one who had lost the bet and had to attend the feast.

The Chief would speak briefly to welcome the people and to say a prayer before the feast began. Then some of the Councillors, with the help of some of the young men, served the food. While the people ate, other young men and women would come around with pails of hot tea or cold water. When the feast was over, the young men would pass around some cigarettes or tobacco to the men. Some of the men would get up and walk to the Chief's tent. There they would smoke the cigarettes and talk among themselves. Meanwhile, the women took some leftover food back to their tents.

Some evenings, many of the young men would get together and organize hand games. There would be about three or four singers and drummers. The rapid drumbeats would attract others, who would gather around the players and watch the games. Quite often, there would be a loud cheer when a player would beat out the opposing player.

The treaty feast was usually followed by a tea dance. The men would start the first few dances and eventually the women would join in. This would continue into the early morning hours. During this time, some of us kids would run around playing tag, hide and seek or some other games. Eventually, we'd get tired of the games and sit by a tent to watch the tea dance. Occasionally, some of us would join in the dances. As the night wore on, the younger ones would gradually nod off. Once, my dad sent my sister over to where I was sitting and she took me back to our tent. My dad remained at the tea dance until it was over.

Our tent was set up some distance from the tea dance area, but I could hear the singing as the dance went on. As I lay on the blankets under the mosquito net, listening to the singing, the songs seemed to come drifting over the grass with the early morning mist. I closed my eyes and imagined that one day, when I was old enough, I would serve at a feast and sing at a tea dance with the other young men my age. I fell asleep listening to the singing.

Once the treaty time was over, the games and tea dances would stop and the settlement was quiet again for another summer.

During the summer, when most of the people were in the settlement for treaty activities, Grandfather had a tent set up behind the Hudson's Bay compound. In the evenings and late afternoons, some of the men would gather around his tent. On warm summer afternoons, the side walls and flaps of his tent would be raised and held in place with short, wooden poles. This provided some breeze through the tent. The men would talk among themselves until Grandfather began to tell his stories. I think he was into his early seventies at that time.

Grandfather's English name was Paul. My brother, Archie, once told me that Grandfather had been Chief of the Fort Providence Indian Band for about twenty-nine years. He had been the third Chief of Fort Providence since treaty was signed in 1921, and retired long before I was born. He had decided to retire mainly because of his age. Over his many years as a Chief and leader, he gained respect and honour among the people; men listened to his stories and to whatever he had to say.

The stories Grandfather told were about our people from long ago, before white men and priests arrived on our land. Some stories detailed his personal experiences as a young man. Others were about individuals who had great powers, or about how they overcame some great hardship through the wise use of their medicine. There were also stories about outwitting other people, especially the Cree Indians, who used to raid camps and kidnap women and children.

Grandfather told a story about a hand game competition among other Dene people who lived along the river somewhere across the big lake. Skilled hand game players and drummers were selected along with several other young men, including two elders. The young men paddled up the river and along the big lake for several days, camping as they went. Finally, they arrived at the area where the games were to take place. There was a large camp set up, with many teepees on the riverbank and many canoes along the shore.

The hand games lasted for several days. Our young men were winning most of the games, much to the chagrin of the opposing teams. Winning most of the games did not put them on friendly terms with some of the local people, so as soon as the games were over, they loaded up their canoes and left immediately for home.

The next day, they noticed another canoe following them in the distance by the shore. The lake was fairly calm, but one of the elders told the young men to put up the sails and point the canoes away from shore. The elder hit the water twice with his paddle and began to sing. The wind came and filled the sails and the canoes sped across the lake.

Grandfather said it was very strange because the lake appeared to be calm in front of the canoes. The young men didn't know what happened to the canoe that was chasing them. When they reached the shore at the mouth of the river and were back in their own familiar territory, the wind died down as suddenly as it had come.

No one said anything about what had just happened. After resting for awhile, the men paddled back to the main camp by Mills Lake (*Tuah*). Grandfather said he had heard stories like this and had witnessed some of these things when he was just a young boy.

When he was telling a story, Grandfather did not use exaggerated movements with his hands or arms. He made small gestures, like tapping the palm of his left hand with his right hand, simulating drumbeats. Sometimes, he would rub his chin with his hand and at the same time point a finger out in no particular direction, to make a point in his story.

Grandfather said the people used to gather in the spring and summer for dances and games, just like they gather now for the treaty celebration. He talked about a particular game the people played but said nowadays, this game is rarely mentioned; it was something people participated in but didn't talk about. The Slavey name for this game is *tsihro*.

Young men were selected and given two eagle feathers, which they placed on their heads. They all carried a short, wooden stave, and wore strips of hide and animal fur around their ankles, knees, elbows and arms. Their faces were completely darkened or decorated with charcoal. When the sun set, the eagle feathers on their heads would bend towards the ground and the young men would go into some kind of trance. The game would get very intense at times, and it was said some of the players actually turned into the animals they imitated.

Grandfather said long ago, the Dene believed animals had spirits. The players were able to change into the animals they imitated because of the power given to them in their dreams by those animal spirits. These games would last for two or three days, until the players stopped from shear exhaustion. When they awoke later, after a deep sleep, some wouldn't remember having gone through this experience.

Grandfather told us we would never find these stories in books. These were our stories and we would learn from them as we grew up. Some of the lessons from these stories would influence how we grew up and how we interacted with other people later on in our lives. Things like this game used to take place among the Dene long before the priests and other white men arrived among us. After they came, things began to change.

The last known *tsihro* game to be played was sometime in the 1930s. Thereafter, the missionaries, who did not understand the culture of the Dene people, banned any such ceremony. I don't think they tried to understand the culture They banned most Dene practices, believing they were sinful acts or witchcraft, and the early RCMP would enforce the ban.

Grandfather said that some Dene men, and even some women, had medicine power (*ʔik'o*) but they rarely used it. Maybe they didn't want to use it and were afraid of it, but other people who were close to them knew they had it. Grandfather told a story about such a man, an elder, who lived at a camp someplace on the Horn River (*K'azhaa Deh*).

"It was during the summer, and all the men were away on a hunting trip. One morning, he took some young boys with him across the river to check some fish traps. While checking the traps, he noticed some movement in the bushes on the shore. When they returned to camp, he told the other elders that they were being watched and they must be very careful with only women and children in camp." Grandfather said that a long time ago, people used to raid each other's camps.

"The Dogribs would raid the Slaveys, and the Slaveys would do the same. Other times, the Cree would raid the camps. During these raids, some people were killed, some women and children were kidnapped, and personal property, like weapons or canoes, were taken."

Grandfather continued his story, "Everyone moved to the teepees on the riverbank, where they could watch the river for any sign of danger. Suddenly, one of the boys jumped up saying, 'Look at those dogs!' and pointed at the river. The old man got up and noticed two dogs swimming towards the camp. The old man quickly grabbed the pouch that hung around his neck and took out a long, shiny, bone needle. He placed the bone needle between his hands and began to sing. Then he stopped singing and blew into his hands, spreading them out as if to release something.

"The swimming dogs began to thrash about in the water. Then dog skins floated to one side to reveal human hands waving out of the water, trying to grab something. They heard some yelling in the bushes across the river and then all was quiet. The old man stood on the riverbank and suddenly, clasped his hands together to his stomach, as if he had caught something. It was the bloody bone needle. He put it back into the pouch that hung around his neck and walked back to his teepee as if nothing had happened."

I was familiar with *K'azhaa Deh,* as we had paddled that river many times. I was also familiar with some of the places along the river. As I sat and listened to the stories, I tried to imagine where some of these events might have taken place.

"This is what they say happened a long, long time ago on the Horn River. Back then some men, even some women, were able to do extraordinary things because they had power, they had medicine power (*?ik'o*)," Grandfather said.

∽

It was in early August when we made our way back to Lishamie from our summer fishing camp. My dad set a fishnet at the mouth of the narrow channel before we continued to the village.

When we finally arrived, we hauled all our things up the riverbank to the house. Then we helped my dad with some of the brush around the house and the outside fireplace area. He used a scythe with a long, curved blade to cut the tall grass and most of the shrubs. We made a fire and collected all the cut grass and various bushes and threw them into the fire. Later, we helped my dad set up a tent close to the house. We would be able to sleep in the tent if it got too warm in the house. The weather could continue to be warm for a few more weeks.

Then a few days later, my dad got very sick. He was lying on the bedding on the tent floor and kept saying he was cold. My sister ran over and got Grandmother. She told us that my dad had a fever, then gave him some rat root and asked him to chew it and swallow the juice.

I sat beside my dad and cried, telling him I didn't want him to be sick. My dad reassured me that he was going to be all right after he had a good sleep, but I continued to cry anyway. I had already lost my mother and I didn't want to lose my dad now. I was scared and didn't know what to do. I went outside and whispered in my language, "Grandfather, if you hear me, please help my dad." I was only eight years old, but at that moment, I was prepared to do anything to make my dad well again. A couple of days later, I was relieved to see my dad was healthy and back to his old self again.

⚬

At this time of the year, there were all kinds of wild berries around our village. Along the riverbank by our house stood some tall saskatoon bushes with ripened berries hanging in bunches, just ready to be picked. Further up by Grandfather's house were patches of raspberry and gooseberry bushes. In the clearings and along the shore were strawberries. Some distance back in the bushes, were large patches of blueberries. Each of the log houses had a trail that led to the nearest blueberry patch.

On berry-picking days, the first thing the men would do upon arriving at the berry patch was look for a large, dry area for a cookout, which we would have later in the day. The area would be marked with a couple pieces of moss or a packsack placed on a large wooden tripod. Next, the men would dig a hole in the moss by hand. The hole was approximately two feet deep and about the same in width. Then they placed spruce boughs at the bottom and on the sides of the hole and left it. During the day as we were picking berries, the hole would slowly fill up with water. The spruce boughs acted as a filter and kept pieces of moss and small twigs from floating to the top.

Berry picking was usually a big family affair. We all helped our mothers to fill one or two large pails or large birch bark buckets. We each had our own cup, pail or small birch bark bowl, which we filled with berries and emptied into a larger container. Sometimes when we picked berries, we would play games, like racing to see who could fill their small container the fastest, or betting on who would last the longest without eating one single berry. We would all lose at this game because, sooner or later, we began to eat berries without thinking about it.

On berry-picking trips, some of the women would cut or tear off large chunks of moss and place them on short spruce trees or willow branches. The moss would eventually dry in the sun and wind. These bundles would be picked up later and the dried moss was used in cloth diapers, similar to modern-day diapers, which are made with cloth and cotton filling. The moss we used between two pieces of cloth worked just as well.

Later in the day, the men would return to the picnic site and make a fire. They took water from the hole in the moss and made tea. The women and children would eventually make their way to the picnic area. There were all kinds of things to cook and eat, including fish (some fresh and some partially dried), moose meat, ducks or spruce hens. The men would place spruce boughs on the ground and cover them with aspen and willow branches. The women would place cooked fish and meat on the branches and everyone helped themselves. Nobody went hungry; everybody ate something.

After the picnic, we mostly just lay around resting and some of us took naps. Then, some of the women went back to picking berries and would fill their remaining containers. When the men picked up these containers and started back to the village, it was the usual signal that berry picking was over for the day, and the women and children eventually followed the men back to the village.

A few days after berry picking, in the early afternoon, my dad left in a small canoe to check the fishnets, just like he did everyday. We played by the shore waiting for his return. Some of us took off our moccasins, rolled up our pant legs and waded in the water, looking for what we called fancy rocks or odd-shaped rocks. Suddenly, one of the boys pointed at a canoe upriver. It was my dad paddling back. He wasn't gone that long and was now paddling as fast as he could. Maybe something had happened.

He landed the canoe, told us to keep quiet and hurried up the riverbank. Shortly, he returned with Uncle Pierre, who was carrying a 30-30 rifle. They got into the canoe, told us to keep quiet again, and quickly paddled away across the channel. We continued playing on the rocks along the shore and quietly talked among ourselves. Once in a while, someone would say, "shh-shh!" in a loud whisper, and we'd all stop what we were doing and listen. We were quiet for a few moments and then we'd go back to whatever we were doing.

Then suddenly, we heard a rifleshot, followed almost immediately by a second shot. The sound echoed in the channel and seemed to crash back into the trees until it faded. Then it was quiet again. Sometime later, the canoe came into sight and when they had landed, my dad told us that they had just shot a moose. We all looked at each other and smiled. We were going to have fresh moose meat!

I followed my dad as he went up the riverbank to the house. I watched as he picked up a couple of knives, a file, a tea pail and other things and placed them into a packsack. Then he picked up the axe and headed back down to the canoe. I followed him down the bank, asking if I could go with him. Uncle Pierre was already waiting by the canoe. I asked again, and finally my dad said that I could go with them. As the men prepared to launch the big canoe, I ran back to the house to get my jacket.

Following the shoreline, we paddled to the mouth of the channel. When we got to the area, I looked along the shoreline for the moose but I didn't see anything. I thought that maybe it had fallen in the tall willows away from shore. We paddled a little further and my dad pointed his paddle at the moose floating in the weeds. Apparently, the moose had waded into the water to feed on the weeds when my dad saw it and hurried back to the village.

My dad reached into the water and lifted the moose's head. He took out a knife and made a cut between the moose's lower jawbones. Through this cut he passed a rope and made a knot. The rest of the rope was passed back to Uncle Pierre, who sat at the rear of the canoe. Then the hard work of towing the moose to shore began.

Once on the shore, we walked into the bushes to collect spruce boughs, and willow and aspen branches complete with leaves. We placed these next to the moose, then walked back to collect some firewood. My dad made a fire and put a pail of water on for tea.

At last, the men turned their attention to the moose, pushing it onto its side on top of the branches as they prepared to skin it. After awhile, my dad called me over and told me to watch and remember. I helped when I could or when I was asked to, and I knew I was learning something important.

They skinned one side, then cut off the limbs. These were placed on a pile of spruce boughs at the shoreline next to the canoe. Then they turned the moose onto its other side, began skinning again and removed the other limbs. Next, I watched my dad clean and prepare the moose's heart. He also cleaned certain parts of the intestines and the kidneys, and turned the stomach inside out, cleaning it in the river. Finally, he placed the liver inside the stomach. We didn't have plastic bags back then, so we made do with whatever we had.

Once the meat was all cut up, we collected more spruce boughs and willow branches and placed them in the bottom of the canoe. The moose hide was placed in the canoe on top of the branches with the flesh side up. After this, the men then placed all the meat on the hide and covered it with more branches. By then it was getting late into the evening. We hadn't noticed that the fog from the main river had slowly begun to move onto shore. Soon, we could barely see the opposite shore of the channel.

My dad and Uncle Pierre agreed to stay for the night rather than paddle in the dark and fog. They didn't want to chance running ashore or over rocks in shallow water. My dad placed a large piece of canvas tarp on top of the spruce boughs and we settled down by the fire. We all lay on the canvas to sleep and covered up with our jackets. t was cold during the night, but I stayed warm sleeping between my dad and Uncle Pierre.

They were both up long before me and had built up the fire. The warmth made me drowsy and I wanted to sleep longer, but I had to get up. My dad had made tea and cooked up fresh moose meat. We took our time eating, as we had to wait for the fog to clear.

At last, it was clear enough and we paddled in the direction of the opposite shore, stopping so that my dad could check his fishnets before we headed back to the village.

In a few days, Josie and I would be heading to the settlement and back to the residential school for another year. I tried not to think about it as we continued back to Lishamie.

CHAPTER NINE

We left Lishamie one early morning, ahead of the other families, paddling up the channel to the Mackenzie River and continuing towards the settlement on the north shore of the river. I watched the shoreline as we passed some familiar places: where we had our summer camp, where my dad had set his fishnets, and where we had picked and eaten berries. Little did I know then that one day I would be running home on this same shoreline.

When we arrived at the settlement sometime in the late afternoon, we came ashore at the usual landing below the Hudson's Bay store. Some other families were already there. The whole scene reminded me of the previous year, when we had arrived at this same place with my parents for my first year at the residential school.

As my dad walked us to the residential school, I began to have this awful feeling in the pit of my stomach. I didn't want to leave my dad again and yet I didn't want him to see me cry, either. I desperately tried to hold back my tears, and put on a brave face. We approached the big, grey building and walked up the wide stairs leading to the parlour area. My dad rang the doorbell, and as before, we all stood together, only this time it was just my dad, Josie, and me. Then, the Sisters appeared and took me away from my dad the second time. But this time, I knew what to expect.

Soon I was back in the recreation area again with the other boys, sitting on the long benches along the wall and waiting for the Sisters. Some of the boys, especially the newcomers, were crying. It reminded me of my first day at the residential school. When the Sisters finally arrived, we all went upstairs to the dormitory; and just as we had done on my very first day at the residential school, we got undressed, put our clothes on our assigned beds and got ready for a bath. After bathing, we put on the old denim coveralls again. And, so I began my second year at the residential school without great enthusiasm.

For the next six years, my life at the Sacred Heart Residential School had its good moments and bad moments. The bad moments were the times I arrived there and the good moments were when I left the place for the summer. After returning from the summer holidays, we all resigned ourselves to the fact that we were there to stay for the next ten months. I guess I was more fortunate than some of the other boys and girls at the residential school because I was able to go home for the summer. At least I could be with my family for brief periods while growing up.

Yet at the same time, being forced to follow a structured life under the strict watch of the priests, Sisters, Brothers, and being afraid to question anything or show emotion, did have an affect on me. Over time, and only after many years, did I realize how much of my own traditions and close family ties had been lost. It is one of the legacies of residential school life.

During my second year at the residential school, my sister, Josie, went away to the hospital. I didn't know what was wrong, as the Sisters never did tell me. They also never told me that she was going away. I only found out about it after she had come back to the residential school.

I normally saw Josie with the other girls during meal times, even though I was never allowed to talk to her. Then one day, she wasn't there. I didn't ask dare where she was. Days went by, and my sister was still missing at meal times. I didn't know what had happened to her. Was she sick? Did she go home to my dad? I just didn't know what to think and was worried I might never see her again.

Then one day, the Sister called me into the building. As usual, I wasn't sure what the reason was for her calling me in, but she told me there was someone here to visit me. She told me to go to the parlour area, where our parents usually waited to see us. I walked over to the parlour but there was no one around, so I sat on the bench and wondered who had come to visit me. Soon, I heard the Sister coming down the hallway, talking to someone. The Sister came in through the doorway, turned around and said, "Look who's here to see you!"

A young girl came into the visiting room. She was neatly dressed and wearing a black beret. She looked at me and called me by my name. Then she said in our language, "It's me, Josie, your sister." I looked up and recognized then that it was Josie! She had finally come back.

I stood up as she took my hand and hugged me. I remained stiff and I didn't return the emotion, as the Sister was standing close by, watching us. I didn't dare show that I was happy to see her again. I wish now that I had expressed my happiness. It would have lifted my spirits. Sadly, at only eight years old, I had already begun to close down emotionally, especially when I was at the residential school.

Josie told me that she had been to the hospital. She didn't say why she had gone and I didn't ask her. Even years later I still don't know why she went to the hospital. I never did ask her and eventually I forgot the whole incident. She asked if my dad had been around for a visit. I didn't say too much because I didn't know what to say or what to ask; she did most of the talking.

Then, a few minutes later, the Sister abruptly said our little visit was over. Josie went back to the girls' section and I walked back to the boys' section. At supper that evening, I saw my sister again with the other girls. Deep inside, I was thrilled to see her again, and happy that she was back to stay.

∽

One winter's day, the Sister called me into the building and told me that I was to travel with the Father Superior to visit some of the camps downriver. I would be leaving with him the next day. I had heard stories about the early missionaries who had made dog team trips to visit camps to give mass, baptize new babies and perform wedding ceremonies. I imagined this trip would be similar to the one made by the RCMP, who made their monthly or quarterly patrols by dog team to and from the various camps. I felt excited and anxious about this trip. I made sure I had warm clothes to wear, as I wouldn't be taking anything with me except what I had on my back. I assumed the Father Superior would make sure we got whatever food and supplies we needed for our trip.

After breakfast the next morning, the Sister gave me a new pair of mitts and an extra pair of socks. When the Father Superior arrived with the dog team, some of the boys ran outside and held the dogs while the others brought up supplies from the kitchen and loaded the toboggan. They placed a couple of packsacks upon two sticks of frozen fish at the front of the toboggan. A box was neatly tied onto the back of the toboggan. I assumed this box held the Father's ceremonial supplies for mass and benediction services. Once it was loaded, I climbed into the toboggan and covered myself with a blanket. The boys let go of the dog team and we were on the first leg of our journey.

We made our way to the place we called One Mile, crossed the Snye, then snaked up the long side slope of the riverbank and overland to the Mackenzie River. The overland trail was pretty rough and the toboggan slid from side to side as the dogs pulled it along.

The Father was standing at the back of the toboggan with a firm grip on the handles. Once in a while, he'd put one foot in the snow and push or steer it, and occasionally he'd run behind the toboggan, holding onto a length of rope.

Finally, we approached the riverbank where the trail ran along the shore of the Mackenzie River. This trail ran through some willows at an incline, which made it easier for the dogs to pull the toboggan up the riverbank or back down it with a full load. The dog team scrambled down the bank cautiously at first, and then broke into full running speed to keep ahead of the sliding toboggan. As the toboggan slid from side to side and around a small bend on the trail, the Father fell off. He stood up immediately and began yelling at me to stop the dog team.

I looked back as the dog team pulled the toboggan and me away from him. It was like looking through a camera lens as it gradually zoomed away from an object. Sitting there on the toboggan, I wasn't quite sure what I should do. I was yelling,

"Whoa! Whoa!" but the dogs weren't listening to me. I was helpless, just as I had been back in Lishamie, when my brothers had put me in that small toboggan and the dogs took off with me. I remembered that those dogs had finally stopped only when the harness caught on the corner of the house, tipping over the toboggan. But at this moment, there was no house in front of me, just wide open spaces. I had to do something quickly.

I thought that maybe if I spilled the toboggan, the dog team might stop, so I swayed my body from side to side as hard as I could, finally tipping the toboggan to one side, creating a cloud of snow. It rode in this position for a few seconds, which seemed like forever, until the dog team slowed down and finally stopped. Snow was packed into the toboggan. My face was covered with snow, and there was more up my sleeves and in my new mitts. I struggled out of the toboggan and brushed myself off.

Soon, I saw the Father jogging up the trail towards me. He stopped by the toboggan to catch his breath. I could see that he was visibly angry and mumbling something about 'sacre bleu' and some other priestly swear words. Eventually, we up-righted the toboggan and put everything back into place. I shook the blanket and put it back in the toboggan, then we climbed on and continued our trip. We arrived at Lishamie without any further incident.

Before we went up the riverbank, I got out of the tobog-gan, and walked behind as the Father drove the dog team up, directly to Grandfather's house. I unsnapped one side of the lead dog's harness and wrapped it around an aspen tree. Later, we would tie up the rest of the dogs in the bushes beside the riverbank.

Back then, most of the people in Lishamie spoke South Slavey; very few could speak any English or French, so I interpreted for the Father as he visited all the houses. He told everyone that he would be hearing confessions in the evening at Uncle Pierre's house. I didn't hear him ask for permission to use the house; he simply commandeered it for the occasion. After the confessions were over, everyone gathered at Grandfather's house for a benediction service. It was not like the benediction services we attended back at the residential school. Here, the people said the rosary and received a blessing from the priest. After the short service, the Father told everyone that he would say mass the next morning in Grandfather's house. Once the people had left, my brother, Daniel, helped me feed the mission dogs. Then we cut some firewood and brought it into the house, being careful not to make too much noise in case the Father was praying or preparing for the morning service.

I hadn't brought any blankets, thinking the Father would have taken care of whatever we needed for our trip. Perhaps the Father didn't know much about what was required for a dog team trip, or maybe he had thought the people would look after us. Daniel gave up his bed for the Father, who put his blankets on the bed. Then, the Father began reading from his breviary by candlelight at the table.

Grandfather gave me some blankets and told me to sleep next to Daniel on the floor by the stove. After awhile the Father climbed into bed and covered himself with his blankets. Then my brother put out the candle. The pale moonlight shone through the window and lit up the room as we all fell asleep. During the night, I heard my brother get up several times to put more wood in the stove to keep the fire burning.

In the morning, Daniel warmed some water in a basin for the Father to wash up. Then the Father began to set up a small table as an altar under a window, as Daniel and I washed up. Soon, the local people began to arrive, filling Grandfather's house. The Father lit two small candles, placed them on either side of his chalice, and proceeded to say mass. I served as the altar boy. During the service, the people came up to the makeshift altar to receive their communion. After the service, the Father put his vestment and chalice away in a box. Once everyone had gone home, we got ready for breakfast. The Father carried his own food, which had been precooked and prepared by the Sisters. From a packsack, he took out some bread, jam and boiled eggs. He sat at the table and began to eat, never offering me anything.

I guess the Father had expected my grandparents or other people to feed me on this trip. I watched as he put jam on a hard-boiled egg and ate it. I thought it a little strange as we usually put salt on boiled eggs and jam on bread. Grandfather made tea and offered me some porridge. He followed that with fried moose meat and bannock. I sat next to him on the floor and ate my food.

After everyone had eaten, the Father announced that we would be going back to the residential school, adding that we would make a trip to the other camps at another time. Soon, we hitched up the dogs, loaded up the toboggan and headed back to the settlement. The return trip was, needless to say, uneventful.

Back at the residential school, life was routine again. Christmas and Easter came and went, and as the spring turned to summer, I was waiting with anticipation for the freedom of being home again in Lishamie.

The newly formed Fort Providence Boy Scouts

CHAPTER TEN

My dad came to pick us up at the residential school when it was finally over for the summer. He had set up his tent next to my grandparents, in the field behind the Hudson's Bay compound. There were many other tents in the field at that time, as the people had gathered to pick up their children at the residential school and to wait for the annual Treaty Day Celebration. It felt great to be back with my family again.

One day, my dad mentioned that we would be spending the summer with Johnny Gargan and his family. I went to the residential school with some of the boys, and knew other members of that family. We would travel to their village at Redknife River, which we called *Ts'udatoah* in our language. We stayed in the settlement until the annual treaty celebration was over and everyone began heading back into the bush to their summer camps.

The Gargans had a large scow and a nine-horsepower kicker. We loaded up the scow with some of our belongings, including supplies, tents, gas and dogs. My dad's canoe was also loaded up and tied next to the scow.

Finally, we headed across the river and made our way along the southern shore to Mills Lake (*Tuah*). A slight wind picked up and created waves on the lake, so we went ashore for the night. The next day, the wind had died down and the lake was calm. After a quick meal, we loaded up the scow and canoe again, then travelled along the southern shore of the lake until we arrived across from Big Point (*Edahro*). From there, we headed across the river to a distant small island we called *Tthe Nduk'a* in our language. There, we all went ashore; the men made a big fire and the women cooked us something to eat. Once we had eaten, we all got back into the scow and headed across to the south side of the river, and from there, we travelled along the shore towards Axe Point.

Axe Point was an old, deserted army camp. It was used as one of the staging areas for supplies needed for the Norman Wells Canol project

We landed below the old army campsite and went ashore. While the men were filling up the gas tank, we walked up the riverbank to explore some of the buildings and equipment. There were Quonset huts situated near the willows and tall aspen trees. Some of the huts had roofs that had caved in from the weight of the winter snow, or from the heavy, wet, melting snow in the spring. Other huts had willows or small aspen trees growing out of the openings in the roofs and the open doorways and windows. There were a few scattered boats left high and dry some distance from the shore, and an airstrip, overgrown now with vegetation. Lots of raspberry bushes lined the edges of the airstrip. We walked among the ruins for awhile before the men called us back to the scow.

Johnny said that we would set up camp at the mouth of the creek across the river and stay there a couple of days as the men planned to go hunting. We headed back across to the north side of the river, landing just upriver from the mouth of the creek. The dogs were let loose and we all went ashore. We unloaded the scow and then cleared out some areas to set up our tents. Soon after the tents were set up, Johnny and my dad left in a small canoe to go hunting up the creek.

Early the next morning, they returned from their hunting trip with moose meat. After a meal of fresh meat, we all set out up the creek in a couple of canoes to bring in the remainder of the kill. Here and there along the shore were freshly cut aspen trees and willow branches. The men told us that these were signs of beaver activity; there probably was a lodge close by.

We kept on paddling and soon landed at a place that my dad and Johnny had marked with a large tripod structure made out of dried aspen poles. Then, each of us grabbed a packsack and followed them into the bushes. I don't know how far we walked, but it was a fair distance. We finally came to a large, open area and followed the men as they walked across the clearing. They stopped at the spot where the rest of the moose meat had been stashed under piles of willow branches and spruce boughs. The men uncovered the meat and built a small fire; the smoke would keep the mosquitoes away. They cut up the meat and we filled our packsacks.

One woman asked me to carry her baby so she could pack out some of the moose meat. She helped me put the baby onto my back and loosely covered the baby's face with a kerchief. Then I followed the others back to the canoes at the creek.

As we approached the creek, there was a sudden commotion up front in the bushes. Someone yelled, "Bees! Bees!" and we all scattered in the general direction of the creek. I moved as fast as I could down onto the shore, followed soon after by the others.

One boy got the worst of the bee stings. His face and eyes were puffed up and he was crying. His grandmother quickly gathered up a handful of leaves from the nearby bushes and began to chew them, spreading them on the boy's face to ease his pain. She said that this would draw out the bee sting venom and bring down the swelling. Later that evening, the swelling had gone down, although his face was slightly green from the leaves for a couple of days.

We stayed by the creek while the women dried some meat and the men set fishnets. A few days later, we broke camp and headed for Redknife River. The dogs were let loose and they followed us along the shore. The Redknife River empties into the south side of the Mackenzie River, and the village was located on the north shore, immediately across from the Redknife River. After travelling for the better part of the day, we finally arrived at the village site. The men landed just below the first of four log houses in the village and began unloading supplies and other gear. The bank leading up to the log houses wasn't as steep as the one back at Lishamie. Its gentle slope made it much easier to walk uphill with a load.

The men cleared an area close to the riverbank and soon the tents were set up. The dogs were caught and tied as soon as they entered camp. Other families arrived and set up tents in front of their respective log houses. Over the next few days, the men went out to set fishnets and collect firewood, while the women continued to dry the rest of the moose meat and fish. The men also spent some time doing minor repairs to the houses. And we, the kids, spent the summer days picking berries, line fishing, swimming and playing improvised games, like kids do everywhere.

One day, some of the women decided to go across the river to pick raspberries and saskatoon berries. They wanted to make a day of it, so we brought along some meat and fish for a cookout. A couple of the younger men went along to operate the kicker. We set out and made our way up the Redknife River, landing some distance inland in a small bay. It was a warm, breezy day, perfect to keep the mosquitoes down.

The women went in all directions; some went to familiar berry spots, others began looking around, hoping to find a good picking spot with lots of berries. There was a dog travelling with us, in case we came across a bear or some other animal. The dog would bark to scare it away and give us enough warning time to get to a safe place or find another person. Soon, everyone had found a spot and was busy picking berries. Suddenly, the dog barked in the bushes and then gave out a muffled cry. One of the men went to check on it, and when he led the dog out of the bushes, the poor thing had some quills sticking out of its chin and nose. Apparently, the dog had found a porcupine and curiosity got the best of him. One of the men put a short rope around the dog's neck and held it firmly on the ground as the other man pulled out the quills with a pair of pliers. The dog's chin and nose swelled up, but in a day or two, it was back to normal again.

After picking berries for some time, the women prepared to have a cookout. The men had already made a fire by the shore and tea was made. Soon, everyone gathered to cook a piece of meat or some fish. After we had had our fill of moose meat and fish some of us took naps, while a few of the women returned to picking berries. They picked into the late evening, and then once again, we set out across the river back to our camp.

The next day, we watched as one of the women spread a large canvas tarp on the shore among the rocks. She then emptied pails of saskatoon berries on the tarp and spread them out with a willow branch. The berries were left like that for the whole day, then everything was picked up in the evening and spread out again the next morning. The berries eventually dried up and were put into birch bark pails, which were then hung in the log houses for future use.

During the summers we rarely saw 'outsiders'. The only people we saw were local hunters or visitors from other communities, so we were surprised one day when two white men arrived in a small canoe. They could have been tourists paddling down the river. Back then, we didn't know anything about tourists. We never expected anyone, least of all white people, paddling the river, and we wondered why they were there. They made camp a distance upriver from where our canoes were tied up onshore. They stayed there for a couple of days and never came over to talk to anyone from our camp. We weren't afraid of them, just a little suspicious.

Then one afternoon, they came over to our camp. One of them had a small package, which he offered to Johnny. He, in turn, gave them some bannock. The package contained some tobacco and a couple of tin cans, which I think contained fruit. The two men asked about the river and how many days it would take to get to Fort Simpson. They didn't say where their hometown was, but mentioned they had started their journey from Hay River and were paddling up to Norman Wells. From there, they hoped to take a plane back to Edmonton. They took some pictures of the camp and a couple more of the log houses, and then walked back to their tent.

The next day, the two men left, one paddling the canoe and the other walking along the shore. After they disappeared behind the point, some of the men from our camp followed them in a large canoe. The men came back after about an hour and said the one white man in the canoe had come ashore and picked up his partner. Then the two men paddled across the river and disappeared behind an island about a mile downriver.

A few days later, most of the men were busy and Baptiste wanted to check the fishnets and hunt for rabbits in the bush across the river. He asked if I wanted to go hunting and I said I would like to go.

Baptiste was a relative of the Johnny Gargan family. I didn't know how old he was, but he was a married man with a couple of children. He had a log house at the Redknife village, where he lived with his family and trapped during the winter. He had an outboard motor on his canoe and we headed across the Mackenzie River.

Once we reached Redknife River, Baptiste shut off the kicker and we paddled a short distance upriver until we reached the fishnets. He said he would check the nets on our way back to the camp. It was quiet as we paddled further upriver and landed by a small point. We pulled up the canoe and tied it to some willows. Baptiste put the packsack on his back and put four or five shells in the chamber of his 30-30 rifle. He asked me to carry it and picked up a .22 rifle. Then I followed him up the riverbank and into the bush.

Once in a while, he would stop and place the top of his right hand over his lips. He moved his hand rapidly up and down over his lips and at the same time blew in and out over his hand. This made a loud hissing noise. Then he'd stop and stand still or kneel on the ground, listened and waited for a few moments. Whenever we'd see a rabbit hopping in our direction, he'd shoot it. We did this for awhile, until he had shot about five or six rabbits.

After some time, we came upon a large clearing and cautiously walked along the edge among the willows. Baptiste stopped and made the hissing sounds again. Suddenly, a large black bear reared itself up about thirty or forty feet in front of us. I was scared and just froze. Baptiste dropped the .22 rifle and grabbed the 30-30 rifle out of my hands, cocked it, took quick aim and fired. It all happened so fast and it was over in a few seconds.

The shot echoed through the trees as the bear dropped with a loud grunt. I then saw what I thought were other bears running off into the woods. Baptiste picked up the .22 rifle , gave it to me and told me to stay put. He reloaded the 30-30 rifle and headed to the area where he thought the bear had fallen.

A few moments later, he signaled for me to come forward. The bear was dead, shot in the head through the nose. I then told him that I thought I had seen two other bears run off into the bush and pointed in the general direction I thought they went. He told me to look up the trees. If they were cubs, they'd have likely climbed the trees to safety after taking off.

I stood still as Baptiste walked around the nearby bush. Suddenly, he whistled at me and pointed up a large aspen tree. There, up in the branches, sat two large cubs. He told me that at this time of the year, August, the cubs were about five months old and would spend all their time eating, getting fat for their big winter sleep. He said that the cubs probably would not make it without their mother. It may seem cruel to shoot bear cubs, but back then, all the Dene people lived off the land. We depended on the animals for food, and nothing would go to waste.

Baptiste circled the tree, took careful aim with the 30-30 rifle and fired. Both cubs tumbled down but one of them got stuck between the branches. We got out of the way as the first cub hit the ground a few feet from us. The other cub was dangling from the branches some fifteen feet or so up the tree. We tried to push it off the branches with a long pole, but the cub was too heavy. Then Baptiste said one of us had to climb the tree, and because I was much lighter than he was, it would have to be me. Baptiste pushed me up the tree and I grabbed one large branch. Then carefully, I proceeded to climb the tree. I was a little scared, not sure if the cub was truly dead, and I just didn't know what to expect.

I climbed on until I got close, and poked the cub with a length of a broken branch. The cub didn't move, so I climbed closer. Then I noticed that its head was wedged between two large branches shaped like the letter V. I got into a position where I could push the head out and shoved as hard as I could, but the head wouldn't budge. Baptist shouted at me to try and lift the cub and at the same time push it out. I tried, but I couldn't lift the cub; it was just too heavy for me.

I waited for a few minutes to catch my breath and think about my next move. After several maneuvers, I managed to get into a sitting position with the main part of the tree between my legs. Hugging the tree with both arms, I pushed on the cub's head with both of my feet as hard as I could. The cub began to swing back and forth a little. I kept pushing until suddenly one of the branches snapped, and down went the cub to the ground as I hung onto the swaying tree.

I climbed down and realized Baptiste was gone. I was about to call out for him when I saw him coming through the willows. He was carrying a small pail of water and offered me a drink. As I drank, he told me the river was not far, so maybe we would drag the bears to the riverbank.

He took out a length of rope and a knife from his packsack

and made a small cut on the hide under the bear's jaw. With the blade, he made a hole between the two lower jawbones, then pushed one end of the rope into the hole and out of the bear's mouth, tying a knot.

He cut a length of dried pole and tied this to the other end of the rope. He got on one side and told me to get on the other; the setup was similar to a wagon hitch. We held onto the dried pole and tugged at the rope until the bear moved forward, then proceeded to pull it to the riverbank. Once we got going it was fairly easy pulling as we dragged the bear over the grass and small willow bushes. Using the same technique, we dragged all the bears to the riverbank, where our canoe was tied up.

After a short rest, we cut and collected a bunch of spruce boughs, willows and aspen branches, which we placed at the bottom of the canoe. Then Baptiste moved the canoe parallel to the shore and tied both ends to some rocks. Next, he made a small ramp with four or five short, dried poles, which he leaned against the side of the canoe. Then, we dragged the bears one at a time up the makeshift ramp and into the canoe. It was hard work pulling and dragging but we finally had all the bears in the canoe.

We paddled out towards the main river and didn't stop to check the fishnets. Baptiste started the kicker and we headed across the river back to the main camp. Most of the kids from the camp were waiting on the shore as the canoe approached the landing area. They all knew we had shot something, as I'm sure they had heard the rifle shots. Once we were onshore, the other men came over and helped take the bears out of the canoe. The men skinned and butchered the bears on the spot and distributed the meat among the families. It had been a long and exciting day for me.

It was during that summer at Redknife when I experienced something I'd never seen before. It was a typical warm summer morning, and the men had returned from checking the fishnets. Most of the women were busy cleaning and preparing the fish to dry by the outside fireplace.

It seemed like another uneventful day, when suddenly, one of the women came running to the fireplace by our tent. She looked very worried and told us that another woman, who had not been feeling well for the last couple of days, had suddenly become very sick. A few of the men and women immediately followed her back to her tent, and I tagged along with some other kids.

The sick woman was lying on the spruce bough floor of the tent, covered with blankets. One of the men told us kids to get out of the tent. We left and stood by the fireplace where the sick woman's son sat next to his wife, his head in his hands. Other people arrived and sat with them around the fireplace. We stayed there and tried to see what was going on, but the adults all stood in the way. Someone mentioned that something should be done for the sick woman. Others nodded their heads or uttered some low sound of agreement.

Suddenly, I heard a woman singing in the tent. The song was more like a chant, but once in awhile, I could distinguish a word here and there.

In her song, the woman asked the men to bring her water and certain items. She continued, asking the men to burn something and bring her the ashes. We strained to see past the adults and into the tent. A couple of men threw some wood into the fire. As the flames got higher, another man burned something, but I couldn't see or smell what it was. An elder told us that children should not be present. Josie and the other older girls came and took us back to our tent. Then another woman came over and told us to be quiet so we wouldn't disrupt what was going on. The singing continued for some time then, abruptly, it stopped.

It was late evening and we could see some of the women walking back to their tents. A few of the men remained by the fireplace outside the sick woman's tent.

My sister and the other girls brought in the bedding and we got ready to sleep. All the while, they kept reminding us to keep quiet.

The next morning, one of the kids woke us up and excitedly told us that the woman was walking around by her tent and didn't look sick anymore. We all looked over in the direction of her tent and saw her serving tea to some of the men as they sat eating by the fireplace.

One of the younger girls asked her mother what had happened. She was simply told the woman was no longer sick. There was no elaborate explanation of what had taken place or what had made her well again.

I often wondered what actually happened in that tent; maybe it was *?ik'o* (medicine power). But whatever it was, I never heard anymore about it. This was the way we lived back then, and life went on as usual in camp.

I also experienced something else that summer. One morning, a few of us kids got together to play hide and seek among the log houses some distance from the tent locations. We went about collecting some of the other kids, and ran up to one girl's tent to ask if she was coming to play with us. The flaps at the opening of her parent's tent were wide open. We could see her sitting in the corner close to the entrance sewing something. When we reached the tent, to our surprise, her mother told us that her daughter was unable to play with us.

"She won't be able to walk for the next few days," her mother explained. "My daughter will probably not play games with you too often from now on," she added. The girl didn't say anything, nor did she look at us. She kept her head down and just continued sewing as we left.

It wasn't until I was in my late teens that I found out what this had been all about. Josie finally told me the girl was going through her first menstruation. In this condition, a girl had to be careful where she went and watch what she did. It was a custom back then that a girl be confined to an area as much as possible during her period. Being young, we didn't know anything about such human conditions back then. No one talked openly about such things. It was a woman's thing and it was up to a mother to talk to her daughter about these things.

Women or girls who were menstruating were not allowed to step over certain things, such as guns, men's belongings, nets strung on the ground for mending or any other thing that was used to provide food. The Dene respected these things because they used them to provide for their families. I remember the Father Superior once asked a woman why she walked around some nets strung on the ground rather than step over them. She tried to explain, but the Father just shook his head and went on his way. It was simply a custom and a tradition that formed part of our way of life.

The summer days seemed to fly by and soon it was time for us to get ready to travel back to the settlement. The time was coming for some of us to return to the residential school. The men decided to leave early and take their time getting back to the settlement.

The next day, we broke camp and left for a place we called *Tthe Nduk'a*. It was a small island on the north shore of the river, just downstream from Big Point. We had stopped there for something to eat on our way down to Redknife River about a month ago. But this time we set up a temporary camp. My dad and Johnny set a couple of fishnets in a small bay off the island.

There were flocks of geese arriving to feed on the island and on the grassy area that stretched to the shore of the mainland. In the afternoon the men went out hunting and shot a few geese and ducks. Later that evening, we had a great meal.

The next day, I watched as my dad and the other men began to make dried smoked goose meat. They would pluck a goose and singe off the remaining down feathers. I watched as they cut up the goose and removed most of the bones. Only the wing bone remained with a large, thick slab of meat. This was cut thinner, then hung to be smoked and dried. I've only seen that done a couple of times since then.

Some years later, when I was working at the settlement, my brother, Daniel, and I came out to *Tthe Nduk'a* on a weekend hunting trip. It was fall and the leaves on the willows and other bushes were starting to turn yellow. I walked around the place where as a young boy I had helped my dad set up our tent. The area looked different. Daniel explained that every spring, the ice pushes the rocks and gravel up the shore, making the shoreline look different every summer. There were still flocks of geese coming in to feed on the island. This time, instead of just watching my dad and the other men, I had my own gun and I shot down some geese.

While we were still camped on the island, a fierce thunderstorm blew in. It began with a light breeze that soon became a very gusty wind. As the evening skies began to darken with clouds, we joined the men in pulling the canoes further up onto the shore. One of the men told us that the thunder was having one of its last storms before heading south for the winter.

"It will make a lot of noise to let you know that it was coming back again in the spring," he said. "The strong wind will also blow most of the leaves off the trees and bushes. The bare bushes make it easy for the moose and caribou to rub off the velvet from their antlers. The wind will also make waves on the river that will break up and loosen the weeds on the lake and the rivers so the water will be clear when the fish begin their fall run up the river." In telling us these things, he was explaining that the Elders always believed that there was a reason for everything.

Late in the evening, the wind eased up and then it began to rain, splashing big drops on the roof of the tent. Then the thunder rumbled loudly across the skies, followed by brilliant flashes of lightning that temporarily lit up the surrounding area.

We ran outside and began running around in the rain, hiding behind some bushes whenever the thunder roared or the lightning flashed. Then we'd run to the next bush and wait for the thunder or lightning. Finally, my dad shouted for us to get out of the rain. We ran back into the tent, which was lit up with a couple of candles. We stood by the warm stove and tried to dry our damp jackets and shirts.

My dad told us that the thunder and lightning we just saw were like big guns shooting and bombs exploding. He went on to say that on the last trip to the settlement, the priest told him that the big war was still going on across the ocean.

Many soldiers and other people were getting hurt and some were dying. We shouldn't really be running around in a storm like this; we could easily get hurt. When I returned to the residential school later that fall, the Sisters told us about the Korean War. Then I remembered what my dad had said about the big war across the ocean.

We all stayed on the island until it was time to return to the residential school for another term. Our parents had delayed the inevitable long enough. They had other things to do to prepare for the coming winter.

Early one morning, we broke camp in preparation to leave for the settlement. We travelled across the river and along the southern shore of Mills Lake, stopping for a meal at the old fishing campsite where the Big Snye flows into Mills Lake, then continuing our journey. By late evening, we had arrived near the settlement and prepared to spend the night. The next day, our parents took their time taking down the camp before travelling to the settlement, and by that evening, we were all back in the residential school.

CHAPTER ELEVEN

When classes began for another year, our teacher asked us to write about what we had done and where we had gone during the summer holidays. I wrote about the hunting trip with Baptiste.

Back then, one of the priests printed what we now refer to as a newsletter. There were a few pages of local community news and some parish announcements. This little newsletter was printed on a Gestetner machine. It was not like a Xerox machine that can spit out several pages a minute, but it did the job. The priest read about my hunting story with Baptiste and printed it in the newsletter. Copies of the newsletter were usually mailed to other communities and parishes, so I'm sure that my hunting story was read by a few people in other communities.

The water level in the Snye by the mission would rise only with the spring run-off, then slowly recede during the summer months. Parts of the Snye would get overgrown with grass and dry up. This allowed the people to walk across to the other side on hunting trips.

During this dry period, the water from the main river flowed down the channel into the Snye to a dead end in some tall, thick grass, just below the place we called One Mile. Further down the channel, the Snye was covered with more tall grass and in some areas, the riverbed was covered with tall willows. What was left of the water gathered in the deeper parts and created pools of water here and there.

In the spring, however, the entire length of the Snye was covered with water. The people who lived in the settlement would set fishnets along its shores. Other people who lived in camps further downriver would paddle up the Snye to the settlement to get supplies. But there are times when Mother Nature doesn't keep to the usual pattern of things.

During one spring break-up, the river ice jammed the mouth of the Snye. The strong current of the river, and the pressure of moving ice. pushed thick slabs of ice on top of each other along the shore. Soon, there were huge, rugged piles of ice the full length of the mouth of the Snye. It seemed as though the mighty Mackenzie River had let out its fury after lying quiet under the ice all winter. With no way for the river water to enter or flow out, the Snye literally dried up.

For those of us who lived at the residential school, the Snye was our swimming area. During the spring, and sometimes in the early fall, we went swimming on weekends. Occasionally, we would go swimming some evenings, depending on the weather and the mood of the Sister.

We didn't have swimming trunks, so the Sister would give each of us a short skirt, like the ones worn by the Romans. We would all change in the bushes and put on these short, flannel skirts. But when we got entered the water, the flannel material did not soak up the water immediately and would float up, exposing our bums or other parts, much to the embarrassment of the Sisters, if they happened to be watching at that moment.

Eventually, the Sisters told us to wet the skirts and wring them out before we put them on. Wetting the short skirt prevented it from floating up as we entered the water; however, there was another problem. Some of the boys would dive into the water, and as they dove, the skirt would slide right off and float to the surface. Then some of us resorted to using our belts or any length of string to keep them from coming off unexpectedly.

This particular spring, when the Snye was dry, the Sisters took us for a walk down to the swimming area. From the top of the riverbank we could see part of the Snye. It was dry from shore to shore, and the riverbed was covered with mud, weeds and other debris. There were only a few shallow pools of water here and there.

We all went down to the shore for a closer look. A few of the boys took off their shoes, rolled up their pant-legs and walked out onto the mud and rocks. Some of them sank into the soft mud up to the knees, but got out with help from the other boys. One of the boys found some whole shells that were closed shut. These were like oyster shells, only a little smoother. We called these 'frog plates' in South Slavey when they were opened or separated. When we happened to find these whole shells, we used to skip them across the water not realizing what was inside. Now we learned that these were a kind of freshwater clam.

The Sisters examined these shells and told us to gather a few more. Whatever we found, we rinsed in the pools of water and gave to the Sisters, who put the clams in their aprons and took them back to the residential school.

The next evening, a couple of the Brothers came with us to the Snye. They built a big bonfire and put a big pot of water over it. While waiting for the water to boil, the Brothers gave us a couple of pails to collect some of the shells. We all went out onto the mud and rocks and started hunting for the shells, which we now called clams.

We felt around in the mud and we were lucky to collect a few, getting mud up to our elbows in the process. The Sister had told us not to get our pants muddy, but it couldn't be helped when we stepped onto the soft mud and sank over our knees. Of course, we got scolded for it, even though the Sister had told us to find some clams. Like other times, it was a no-win situation.

We put the clams into the pails and brought them up to the Brothers, who rinsed off the shells again in a small pail of cold water and then threw them into the boiling pot of water for a few minutes. Then, one of the Brothers took out some of the cooked clams which had opened up and he showed us how to eat them. This was something entirely new to some of us. We didn't have any butter or salt but a few of the brave boys tried eating the clams. I decided to try one. The first one I tried didn't taste very good, as there was a little bit of sand in it. The second one I tried was much better, but I didn't eat any more.

As the spring weather warmed up and the days got longer, the big ice jam at the mouth of the Snye slowly melted away. Water eventually flowed back into the Snye, and much to our great delight, we could go swimming again!

∽⊚

One spring weekend, when the ice had melted or floated away from the Snye, the Sister told us that we would make fish-hooks and try our hand at fishing with a line. She produced a bundle of single hooks, passed them around and proceeded to show us how to make fishhooks. She tied two or three single hooks together with some strong fishnet twine. We crowded around her and watched as she made the first fishhook. Then we started making them on our own.

We used a short length of snare wire for a leader and threaded a couple of beads on it. Then we made spinners that we cut from tin cans. We placed the tin spinner in between the two beads on the leader wire and gave it a slight twist, which allowed it to spin in the water. Once we completed our hook, the Sister gave us a length of twine. The homemade fishhook was then tied to the twine and ready for a tryout.

One evening after supper, we all went down to the Snye to try out our fishhooks. We stood on some rocks, swung the hook overhead a few times and cast off the line. Some hooks worked just fine with the first cast, the spinner spinning like they were supposed to, but others needed more adjusting. No one caught a fish that first evening.

The next evening we all went out again back to the Snye and to try our luck again with our homemade fishhooks. One of the other boys was with me that evening. We walked along the shore, looking for a rock large enough to pile our fishing lines on without getting them tangled. I found a large, flat rock, stood on it and began to fish. The other boy walked a little further down the shore looking, for another large rock to fish from.

A few yards upstream, I noticed a fishnet that was tied to a large rock on the shore. There were two long poles tied end to end with the net attached to them. These poles were used to push the net out into the water away from the shore. Once the fishnet was set, the poles were tied to a secure place onshore.

The poles were pulled back onto the shore whenever the net was checked for fish. This method was used especially during the early spring, as soon as there was an opening in the ice along the shores.

The other boy was downstream a short distance from me. He was standing on a large rock, throwing his line out and bringing it back with a hand over hand motion. I was doing the same thing, hoping to catch a fish. Neither one of us got a bite, but we kept trying to catch the big one.

Then I noticed a movement on the fishnet closest to the shore. Something had moved the pole and created a small ripple across the water. I yelled at my friend and he came over. We watched the pole and it moved again. There definitely was a fish in the net.

Then an idea hit me. Why not take the fish out of the net, place the hook in its mouth and say we caught it? It was worth a try; after all, we were after fish. I mentioned the idea to my friend and he nodded in agreement. We looked around to make sure no one was watching us. Then, with my friend hanging onto my belt, I leaned out over the water and took hold of the pole. I pulled the fishnet to the shore until I saw the fish. It was a fair-sized pike and in no time I had it out. Then we pushed the fishnet back out into the water.

I held the pike around the head and pushed the hook into its mouth with a small stick. Then I ran with it along the shore some distance down from the fishnet. I stopped on a large rock and in one motion threw my line, with the fish hooked on, into the water as far as I could. Then my friend started yelling, "Fish! Fish!"

Suddenly, from nowhere, the other boys came running over and gathered around as I slowly brought in my line with the stolen fish at the other end onto the shore. The fish did its part. It started flopping up and down like a fish is supposed to, and the boys moved back a bit to make room for it. I grabbed the fish and hit it a couple of times on the head with a small rock.

Then I took it, with the hook still in its mouth, to the Sister, who by this time had come to the edge of the riverbank with some of the other boys. The priest also came over to look at my fish. After looking at the fish for awhile, he said that it looked like it had been caught in a net. I immediately said it could have been, as I was fishing close to one of the fishnets. To my surprise, he just nodded his head and continued looking at my fish. I think he actually believed me.

I was one of the few boys who did get a fish, although I got mine through other means rather than a fishhook. The Sister brought the fish back to the kitchen at the residential school and I don't remember what happened to it. But at least I can say it's the one that didn't get away, and the experience gave me an original fish story to tell over the years.

The Boys' Shack Sacred Heart School, Providence, N.W.T

Posing before our improvised archery contest

CHAPTER TWELVE

The summer holidays had come and gone, and once again, like all of the other boys and girls, I was back at the residential school for another year. I was ten years old and attending my fourth year at the residential school. Although being there was nothing new to me, I still faced every September with a mixture of anxiety and resignation.

I would usually get a little homesick for the first few days after returning to the residential school, but this time for some reason, I was very homesick. I thought about home just about every day, and I really missed my dad and my grandparents. I could picture the people from my village at their fishing camps, stocking up on white fish for the winter. I pictured my dad going out to check the rabbit snares and fishnets. I really missed going with him on these trips.

It was early on morning around the middle of September, when the Sister woke me up to serve as an altar boy for the first morning mass at six o'clock. I got up, put on my clothes and made my way to the wash area. As I walked past one of the windows, I noticed the clear blue skies in the early morning light. It was going to be a nice, sunny day, and I thought again about my dad at our fish camp.

I washed up, combed my hair, and then walked out of the dormitory. What happened next was really unplanned. I went all the way downstairs to the ground floor and simply walked out the back door into the boys' yard. Once outside, I stood against the wall, wondering what to do next. I walked along to the front of the building and straight out the front gate. Outside the gate, I immediately crouched behind the hedge-covered fence. From this position, I could see the stovepipe sticking out of the pumphouse roof below the riverbank in front of me. I looked around and then ran towards it, scrambling quickly down the makeshift stairs to the landing by the pumphouse and then hid behind the building. It was the start of my "great escape."

After waiting for a short while, I went further down to the shoreline and walked towards some canoes tied up at the familiar spot below the Hudson's Bay store. As I got close to the canoes, I noticed two people covered by their blankets and sleeping by a fireplace. I looked around and spotted a small canoe. I tiptoed over, lifted the small canoe and carefully put it into the water. I was trying desperately not to make any noise. Occasionally, I glanced in the direction of the sleeping men while I slowly pushed the canoe into the water. It was a little too heavy for me but I was determined to get out of there. Finally, after what seemed like a very long time, I got the small canoe into the river, and then took a paddle from another one.

I still didn't want to make too much noise, so I floated the small canoe a few yards downstream before I got in and paddled away. I stayed close to the shore, as I was afraid that I would get carried away by the swift currents, and I never looked back. I paddled past the barge docking area and straight across the Snye to the point of Mission Island.

Once I rounded the point, I knew no one would be able to see me so I relaxed a little, staying as close to the shore as I could dare. A few times, I felt the canoe slide over some rocks in the shallow water. I was scared and hoped the canvas wouldn't tear on a sharp rock. I didn't know what time it was, but it was getting lighter and warmer as I paddled on.

I was about halfway to Lishamie, when I heard the sound of a kicker in the distance, coming from the direction of the settlement. I knew then that they must be out looking for me. I was so scared that I started to cry, and I looked along the shore for a place to hide. The sound of the kicker got louder as it drew nearer. I paddled as fast as I could into some tall grass in a small bay. I didn't have time to get out and run into the bush so I lay down in the canoe. I closed my eyes and hoped that it was not the police.

I waited until the noise faded, and I didn't dare look up until I was sure they were some distance downriver. When I looked up, I noticed a large canoe, but this one did not have the telltale colours of the RCMP. It may have been some of the Signal Corps men going on a duck-hunting trip to the Mills Lake area. I peered out of the canoe occasionally until I saw the canoe disappear around the island. Then I lay down again and waited for a few more minutes, but it seemed like eternity as I listened to the fading putt-putt of the kicker.

Finally, I pushed offshore and paddled a short distance downriver. I landed by a small point, pulled the canoe onto shore and ran into the bush. I sat by some willow bushes and listened for any sound. It was quiet except for the occasional chatter of a squirrel and the quacking of ducks along the shore.

It warmed up as the sun rose higher in the sky and I decided to walk to Lishamie. I thought that once I arrived at our village, I would yell across the narrow channel for someone to pick me up.

As I headed along the shore, I stayed as close to the bushes as I could. This way, if another fast boat came by, I could run into the bushes and hide. As I was walking, I noticed someone in a canoe some distance downriver. Immediately, I ran and hid, then stood on my tiptoes to peek over the bushes to see if I could recognize who it was. Then I carefully moved along the bushes in the direction of the canoe. As I got closer, I saw a man checking fishnets and realized it was my dad! I was so relieved and happy to see it was him.

I walked close to the shore and called out, "*Aba, Aba!*" which in our language means "Father, Father!" or "Dad, Dad!" My dad stopped for a moment and listened, then he shook his head and continued checking the fishnets. He acted like he must have been hearing things. He certainly didn't expect me to be there on the shore. I called out again. He took his pipe from his mouth, tilted his head and seemed puzzled by the sound. I ran up closer and yelled again. This time, he looked up towards the shore and saw me.

Immediately, he paddled to shore and landed his canoe. He picked me up and placed me in the canoe without saying a word, and in a few minutes we were on our way back to the village. I was a little confused; I thought he would be happy to see me, but the concerned look on his face told me otherwise.

When we arrived at Lishamie, my dad took me directly to Grandfather's house. Grandmother took me into the house and began to prepare something for me to eat, while my dad sent my brother over to get my Uncle Harry. In a few minutes, my uncle arrived, followed by my aunt. Looking very worried, he asked if my cousin, Jim, was all right. I just nodded my head. Then he asked if Jim had followed me and I told him I thought he might have. I knew Jim hadn't followed me – he was still in bed when I left the dormitory – but the words just came out. Maybe I didn't want to be the only one in this predicament; I needed an accomplice. My dad stood in front of me.

"You could have drowned if the canoe had capsized," he began. "You could have gotten lost if you had run too far into the bushes; you could have been attacked by some wild animals; you could have gotten hurt, broken a leg or something."

I began to cry. All this time, Grandmother was holding my hand and saying things like, "He's hungry; let him eat something." She was being very protective. Then my dad gave me a pat on the head and told me he probably would have to take me back, but for now, we'd wait and see. I stopped crying, relieved that I wouldn't have to go back to the residential school right away. I went with Grandmother and she fed me. For the better part of the day, I stayed close to my grandparents' house.

It was sometime during the late afternoon, when we heard the sound of the RCMP speedboat. As it appeared around the point and came up the channel, I had this awful feeling in my stomach. I began to cry and ran into Grandfather's house. I was sure I would go to jail for running away from the residential school; that is what scared me the most. My dad reassured me that everything was going to be fine and that he was going to talk to the police. He promised to come with me if the police took me back to the residential school.

Apparently, the police officer and his interpreter had gone to the area further downriver, where we had our summer camp, assuming that the family was still there. The young policeman asked me a few questions. After exchanging some words with my dad, the policeman told me that he had to take me back to the residential school. The news started me crying again. The young policeman was very friendly under what I imagine must have been an awkward situation for him. He was not at all what I had initially expected; that was what had really scared me about the police: the fear of not knowing what would happen when they came for me.

I got my jacket, and we all walked down the riverbank to the RCMP boat. The policeman asked my dad about fishing conditions and duck hunting, using small talk to ease the situation. We all piled into the boat and headed back to the settlement.

Our arrival at the residential school must have been quite a sight, like the return of an escaped criminal. Some years later I saw a movie called *Cool Hand Luke*, starring Paul Newman. The Newman character was in a chain gang and kept running away and getting caught. This movie reminded me of my running away from the residential school. As I followed my dad and the policeman towards the big, grey building, it seemed like all eyes were on me. I imagined everyone was looking at me through the windows.

The Sisters were in the parlour area as we arrived, and so was my sister, Josie. She came over and stood beside my dad and me. The Father Superior came by and spoke to the policeman for awhile. Then he came over and spoke to my dad in French. He patted me on the head and said something like, "Oh, nothing is going to happen to him." Josie spoke to my dad for awhile, until a Sister led her away to the girls' section of the building.

A few moments later, the Father led my dad and the policeman to the parlour door and they walked out. The Father closed the door behind them, then took my hand and roughly led me down the hallway to the boys' section of the building. He pulled a table to the centre of the room and told me to get on it, then called the rest of the boys to gather around.

In a loud voice, he announced, "This boy ran away from here because he doesn't like being taught by the Sisters; he doesn't like getting up in the morning to go to mass; he doesn't like to serve mass; he doesn't want to go to school; he doesn't like to live here," and so on. The Father was trying to make me feel guilty and ashamed, but I didn't feel guilty at all.

Then he asked me why I ran away. I simply told him that I had been homesick, and that I missed my dad and wanted to go home. He looked up at me and shook his head. I stood on the table in tears, not knowing what to do. It seemed like I was there for a very long time. The Father was determined to make an example of me, but it seemed like he really didn't know how to deal with the situation. I think he was actually embarrassed that a ten-year-old boy had run away from the residential school.

Eventually, I was told to go upstairs to bed and to think about the bad thing that I had done. I really didn't think running away to be with my dad and grandparents had been a bad thing. I did not feel I had committed a sin. One of the Sisters came over and told me to get off the table. She grabbed my arm roughly, pinching me as she led me to the door. It seemed like she really wanted to physically hurt me, maybe because she had been the one who woke me up to serve as the altar boy that morning. I think she restrained herself because the Father Superior was present.

As she pushed me towards the stairs, she asked if my dad had been happy to see me. I said no, and that he had been upset about the whole situation. This seemed to satisfy her. In broken English she said, "Good, if he happy to see you, he is a bad man."

I thought to myself, "Why would my dad be considered a bad man if he had been happy to see me?" It didn't make sense to me. For my penance, I had to go to mass for the next few days and I was not allowed to attend special events, like movies.

I thought I was the only boy in the history of the Fort Providence Residential School to ever run away, but years later, I mentioned my story to an Elder. I was told that two young Brothers had run away from the residential school years before I did. They had made their way down the river and were caught somewhere close to Fort Simpson and brought back. There may have been others who tried to run away, but I never heard about anyone else running away after I did. As for my little escapade, no one ever said anything about it again. It was eventually forgotten and life went on as usual at the residential school.

∽

The following spring, after my great escape, I got terribly sick. I remember it was in early May when most of the snow was gone. There were puddles of water here and there in the fields by the residential school. I didn't know it then, but it turned out to be the flu epidemic, and I was one of the first to get it.

It all began with a headache that grew worse, then came a feeling of nausea and wanting to throw up. I went to the Sister to tell her that I wasn't feeling well. She took my temperature and told me that I was okay. I thought then that a thermometer was a device used to measure headache pain and not the temperature of your body. Little did I know about modern medical equipment. When I tried to tell her that I, indeed, had a really bad headache, she just waved me away with her hand.

I sat on one of the benches against the wall with my head in my hands and cried. I thought about my dad and it made me long for my dad and the comfort I knew he could provide. I knew he wouldn't have treated me like the Sister had done.

Suddenly, I felt this awful wave of nausea and I just threw up right where I was sitting. That's when the Sister decided to send me upstairs to bed. The proof that I was really sick was now spread on the floor in front of her.

I stayed in bed for the next few days, and soon other boys started to get sick and were sent to bed. Eventually, the dormitory filled up with sick boys. The few lucky ones helped the Sisters care for the sick boys and brought in the food from the kitchen. There was no such thing as fresh fruit back then. The Sisters gave us slices of dried apples or apricots, which we called 'dried ears.'

During this time, I often thought about my dad and grandparents and wondered how they were doing in Lishamie. I wondered if any of them were sick with the flu. It worried me, and I cried sometimes when I thought about them. The Sisters didn't say anything; they probably thought I was crying because I was feeling sick.

I remembered one of Grandfather's stories about another big flu epidemic that happened when he was a young man. He said many people got sick after receiving some blankets from the Hudson's Bay and the government agent. Many people died during that time. Years later my Uncle Jean, who lived at the seniors' home in Fort Providence, also talked about the blankets and the big flu.

Grandfather said that the people used to gather in the late summer and hold dances, hand game competitions and other traditional games. A great medicine man lived among the people at that time. He had a special drum, and when he used to sing while beating his drum, sometimes black spots would appear on it. The spots would be counted, and he would say that at the next spring gathering, that same number of people would not be around.

One summer at the treaty celebration, the government agent gave out blankets to the people, along with money and shells. At the gathering later that summer, the medicine man sang with his drum, just as he had always done, and as he sang, black spots began to appear on his drum. But this time, the spots covered his entire drum, making it appear black. The medicine man drummed all day and all night, but still his drum stayed black. Then he told the people that something was out there, something stronger than him, and that he didn't know what it was.

Some of the people returned to the bush because they were afraid and didn't know what would happen. Soon, people began to get sick. Over time, more people fell sick; sometimes, entire families died. This was the beginning of the first flu epidemic. The flu spread among the people and the medicine man was among those who died.

I was in bed for a very long time, and finally one day, the Sister took my temperature and told me that I was well enough to get out of bed. I still felt a little weak, but I got out of bed because she told me to do so. For the better part of that day, I sat in the recreation room and looked out the window.

The next morning, the Sister woke me up and told me to serve as altar boy for mass, so I got up and went to the chapel. During the service I felt weak and tried to stand with my legs apart to keep my balance. Whenever I knelt down, I sat on the heels of my feet to rest.

When the Mass was over, the priest said he was giving communion to some of the sick boys and girls. He retrieved a chalice full of host from the altar and handed me a small silver plate and a bell. Then, I followed him up the stairs to the girls' dormitory. Before he entered the dormitory, he looked at me and nodded. I rang the bell I had in my hand. The Sister had prepared a small table with two lit candles by the doorway. The priest placed the chalice on the table and began to say some prayers.

I knelt by the doorway and rested on my heels. I didn't look around during the short service; I just kept my head down and looked at the floor. I didn't want the Sisters to think I was looking at the girls in some provocative way, although they were in their flannel pajamas that stretched from their necks to the floor. After the priest gave communion to the girls, I followed him into the boys' dormitory and he performed the same service. After the service, I went straight back to bed, sick all over again.

The flu lasted until well into the month of June. I was one of the first ones to get sick and I think I was one of the last ones to get out of bed. I don't remember anyone at the residential school who died during that epidemic. The flu had spread into the settlement and even into some of the villages; everyone was affected by it.

Some years later, I spoke with an Elder about the flu at the residential school. She told me about her stay there; she and her brother had arrived at a very young age in the 1940s, and she remembered some of the children getting sick. She said some of them disappeared, their bodies eventually brought out for burial in the spring. Back then, it was too hard to bury someone in the winter when the ground was frozen solid. She remembered about four or five small bodies wrapped in blankets, and that there had been a funeral service for the children. Some parents were not aware of their child's passing because they all lived out on the land back then. They only found out when they came to the residential school to visit their children and the priest had to tell them the bad news.

Visiting day at the Sacred heart School, Fort Providence, N.W.T.

CHAPTER THIRTEEN

The years passed, but my summers were spent with family, breaking the monotony of a long ten months at the residential school. Although most days were routine: school Monday to Friday, chores every day, church services on Sundays and other special occasions; there were also some fun times.

For recreation, we played all kinds of games, some we made up ourselves.

There was a big slide in the boys' yard. The slide was there when I first arrived at the residential school. The girls also had a similar wooden slide.

The one in the boys' yard was built out of logs and stood some ten to twelve feet high. After the first good snowfall, the Sister would have us haul snow up and pack it down the full length of the slide. Then we brought water in pails, which the Sister would pour onto the snow we had packed on the slide. Once the wet snow froze hard enough, we'd use it all winter, occasionally adding more water to ice up the slide surface.

We also slid down the bank of the ravine by the barn. The bank ran in the shape of a large semi-circle from the mission warehouse, along by the barn, on by the graveyard and all the way to the Snye. The bank varied in height all along its full length.

One day, the mission received an assortment of skis, which

the Brothers brought over. Where these skis came from I don't know, they were most likely donated to the mission. Some were short skis, about five feet in length and about four inches wide. Others looked more like cross-country skis: a little longer and narrower. There was a small slit in the middle of each ski that just fit a single strap. The strap was placed over the toe of your moccasin, mukluk or boot and kept your feet attached to the skis.

Like anything new, the skis were great fun and a challenge. We all had our turns using the skis to make a run down the bank of the ravine by the barn. At first, we would go straight down the hill, trying to keep our balance. We didn't move from side to side like regular skiers do; we simply got on the skis and went straight down, nothing fancy. If we fell, we'd get up and try again.

Later on, as we got better at controlling the skis, we'd make long incline runs down along the bank of the ravine. We even piled some snow, packed it down and used it for ski-jumps. They were only two or three feet high, but that was high enough to make you hurt when you landed on your backside.

Some of the boys used slabs from the sides of old wooden barrels. These slabs were tapered at both ends and were about two feet long and about three to four inches wide in the middle. A few boys nailed a small piece of board into the middle of the slab to keep their feet from sliding forward. We also used these on our runs down the makeshift ski-jump. I think we really invented the modern-day snowboard, with our old wooden barrel slabs. Too bad we never knew about patents back then!

We didn't have wax, nor did we know then that one used

wax on the bottom of one's skis. We simply melted some snow in our mouths and then smeared it on the bottom of the skis, just like we did with the runners of our sleds. After it froze, it worked just fine. Most of the boys had wooden sleds, made up of two runners and a couple of pieces of board nailed over the top to keep it together. Sometimes we had races, sliding down the hill to see who went the fastest and the furthest.

We also had "dog-team" races. We'd collect pieces of string, twine, or rope, anything to make a length of strong rope, which we would tie to the sled. With one boy riding the sled, we'd have about six to eight others pulling. We'd run all over the yard with the boy hanging onto the sled as best he could and yelling at us to go faster. The rider fell off more often than he stayed on.

It was in early winter, after snow had covered the ground, when the Sister told us in broken English that we were going to build a skating rink. We usually skated on the Snye once it froze over, but after the snow fell, we didn't skate again until the next fall freeze-up.

The Sister had us shovel snow into a small, level area between the residential school building and the priests' residence. We cleared an area that was smaller than a regular-size skating rink. Then we gathered some wooden planks from one of the Brothers. These were about eight to ten inches wide, two inches thick and varied in length. We placed the planks length-wise, one at a time, on the frozen ground against the snow banks all around the rink. These planks formed the short walls of our new skating rink.

After all the planks were in place, we hauled pails of water from the residential school, which the Sister poured onto our little rink surface. The water flowed this way and that over the uneven ground as steam slowly rose into the air. We continued hauling pails of water and the Sister kept pouring them until the whole rink surface was covered with water. Overnight, it froze in a rough, uneven surface and the next day, we watered the rink again. We waited anxiously for another day until the ice froze evenly and was ready for use. Then we began skating on our little rink and had a great time.

We had no real hockey sticks back then, so some of the boys made their own, nailing a short piece of narrow board to a length of stick. One Sister even showed us how to play hockey. At least, she showed us how she thought hockey was supposed to be played. She spoke mainly French and was from Quebec, so surely she must know what hockey was all about, we thought. Our hockey games, however, were rather disorganized.

We used our little skating rink most every day, well into the cold winter months. Then one day in February, a warm wind blew across the snow in the yard. The Brothers called the warm wind a Chinook. It blew all day and even melted some of the snow. We watched as part of our little rink slowly began to melt away.

We removed the planks, some of which had begun floating around in the water that had gathered at the far end of the rink. It was a good thing we did. Within the next couple of days, the weather changed and turned very cold. Much to our delight, our little rink froze over again, and once again, we were right back out playing more disorganized hockey.

On rainy days, we usually played inside. On some of these occasions, the Sister would make us sit on the benches along the walls and we'd play whatever games she happened to come up with. One I remember was the *"debus-assi"* game. This was French for "stand up and sit down." The object of the game, which was similar to "Simon Says", was for us to stand when she said *"debus"* and to sit when she said *"assi."* She would say these words over and over, as we stood and sat, stood and sat. Sometimes she would try to fool us by saying the same word twice in a row. When that happened, those who were doing the opposite were out of the game. This game got boring after awhile, but we played because the Sister wanted us to.

It was during one of these games that one of the boys, Robert, was just goofing off. The Sister noticed him acting up but she continued the game. After awhile, she walked over, grabbed him by the arm and dragged him across the floor to the door. She let go and threw him onto the floor. As he tried to get up, she kicked him in his side. Robert yelled in pain and began to cry. He stayed crouched on the floor and couldn't move even if he wanted to.

The Sister was about to kick him again when in walked Father Superior. He looked over at the Sister and then he looked over at us. The Sister stood there with Robert at her feet. Robert held one arm protectively over his head and held his other arm around his side, as if expecting a slap or another kick. The Sister, visibly blushing, explained to the priest that Robert had been misbehaving and not listening, so he was being punished. The priest looked at him, shook his head and went out of the room.

Then the Sister looked down at Robert and pointed to the benches. He slowly got up and walked back to his usual place on the benches along the wall. I think the priest was embarrassed for walking in on the Sister. It appeared like he really didn't know what to do or how to react to the situation.

During one of these rainy days, we were all playing inside when one of the Sisters brought in a large piece of canvas. She spread it on the floor and told us that we could wrestle on it if we wanted to, but only two boys at a time. We had a great time wrestling and trying to push each other off the canvas. It was very difficult to do because the canvas moved in whatever direction you happened to move. Some of the boys tried to help by holding down the corners of the canvas, but they only got in the way of the wrestlers.

One of these wrestling matches was between two older boys who were pretty evenly matched. Each was trying desperately to push the other off the canvas. Some of us were standing around cheering them on. Finally, one of them grabbed the other from behind. With both arms around the other's waist and one leg hooked under the other's leg, he used his entire body to push the other off the canvas. He wasn't having too much success but he kept on trying.

Suddenly, the Sister grabbed the boy who was on top by the shirt collar and yanked him back. She yelled that he was doing a bad thing, acting like a dog. The boy stood up with a surprised look on his face. The other boy lay on the canvas looking up, like he was waiting for some explanation.

She kept saying that they were acting like dogs. I guess in her mind, their actions resembled those of mating dogs. This was the furthest thing from our minds. We were too busy watching and enjoying the wrestling match to think of anything else, least of all mating dogs. I think her reaction surprised all of us.

We quit wrestling for the day and amused ourselves with

some other games.

Later on, I thought to myself, did the Sister commit a sin by thinking of a bad thing like mating dogs? They always told us that is was a sin to have bad thoughts. After all, she had been the one to think of the wrestling match as the actions of mating dogs, so had she committed a sin? Maybe she hadn't committed a sin because she was a nun. This is the way I came to think about things like this, especially after being taught religion every day.

Thereafter, we had to be careful of how we wrestled with each other. Eventually, the piece of canvas tore up from use and we all lost interest in this sport. After all we really didn't want anyone else to think that we fought like mating dogs.

ᘈᔆ

One spring day, the Sisters told us that the local RCMP officers were coming to the residential school to teach us some exercises accompanied by music. This was to be our introduction to the new concept of Physical Education in school.

The officers came into our recreation area with a box and some large rolled-up papers. They introduced themselves and opened the box, bringing out a record player and some records. One officer unrolled the papers, which turned out to be some exercise charts, and went on to explain that these exercises were performed by the soldiers in the army, accompanied by military music.

They had a large board made from what we referred to then as beaver board, which they hung on the wall and pinned the charts to. The charts consisted of numerous figures. The officers explained that each figure depicted an exercise position. They asked us to memorize these, as we would be doing these exercises. Over the next while, we learned the various positions, performing them over and over again until we assumed the correct position of any figure the officers pointed to.

Then one day we did the exercises to the beat of the military music. It certainly was a welcome change, and a whole lot better than the *"debus-assi"* game. Eventually, we got better at doing these musical exercises and moved outside into the boys' yard where we had more room to move around. We even performed a special demonstration for the Bishop when he visited the mission. One of the priests, Father Leising, the Bishop's pilot, had a movie camera and filmed us as we performed the musical exercises in the boys' yard.

A few years later, when I was at the mission school in Fort Resolution, I saw the film. The local Father Superior was showing some home movies, and, as it turned out, he had the film of our musical exercises from Fort Providence. As I watched, I thought it looked pretty silly. No one had explained what it was all about. There was no sound either, just a bunch of guys doing exercises that looked like early morning stretches. There didn't appear to be any kind of enthusiasm, either, except from the Bishop, who clapped his hands once in awhile and was all smiles.

In the fall, we piled the firewood at the far end of the boys' yard. The Brothers would cut some green wood in the winter, leave it to dry during the spring and summer and haul it in by horses in early fall. Sometimes, if it wasn't too far away, the Sisters would let us visit the Brothers at their wood camp. They would give us tea and some buns, which we heated on top of the wood stove. We really enjoyed ourselves on these visits. It reminded me of being back home in a camp on the trapline.

Long lengths of firewood were hauled back by a team of

horses to the residential school, unloaded and piled in the far end of the boys' yard. Later, these would be cut into stove lengths for the kitchen and the boiler room. When it was time to cut and pile the wood, one of the Brothers would drive the old tractor to the cutting area. The tractor had steel wheels, rather than rubber tires. We could hear the screeching of these steel wheels over the sound of the engine as the tractor made its way across the boys' yard.

The Brothers brought out a large circular saw, which they placed on a long, heavy table. Then they stretched a length of heavy-duty strap from the tractor to the saw table and put it over a cylinder that turned the saw blade. When the tractor was running in neutral, it would engage the strap, which in turn spun the saw blade.

The Brothers would do the cutting and the hired men would throw the cut wood into a huge pile. This went on for most of the day. The whining of the saw blade droned on as we carried off the cut firewood to an area by the fence where it was put into rows according to length. Short ones, about a foot and a half, for the kitchen; and four-foot lengths for the boiler room. Sometimes, we'd have three or four rows of newly cut firewood running the length of the boys' yard. We also collected sawdust in gunnysacks, which the Brothers hauled away and stored in the cellars under the priests' residence and the work shop.

One day while we were piling the firewood, one of my friends got into an argument with some of the other boys. The noisy quarrel turned into a shoving match and eventually into a wrestling match on the ground.

The Sister hurried over, blowing on her whistle. I happened to be standing next to my friend, Fred, as she came over. Pointing at the two of us, she told us to go into the building. I tried to explain that I hadn't been in the fight, but she just waved us on into the building.

Once inside, she scolded us and said that we shouldn't be fighting in front of the Brothers and the hired men. Again, I tried to explain that I wasn't involved in the fight, but she wouldn't listen, insisting that we had done a bad thing.

I guess she thought we had created a bad impression in front of the hired men from town. For our punishment, we were to clean the washroom in the boys' recreation area.

Once in the washroom area, we got a mop and a pail out of the closet. While I was filling the pail with water, Fred looked my way and smiled. The Sister reacted to this by slapping him across the face. Immediately, he put his left arm up across his face and turned to the wall. There, on the wall directly in front of him, was a mirror. As he looked up from underneath his arm, he saw himself in the mirror and smiled again.

The Sister saw this and hit him across the back with the handle of the mop, which snapped in half. This made her even angrier, and she ordered me to get the saw from the cupboard. I didn't know what she was going to do with the saw, but I hurried to the cupboard and returned with one. She told us to saw the broken piece off the mop handle, which we did. Then she ordered us to start cleaning up. We proceeded to wash and scrub the sink, the toilet bowl and floor with the short-handled mop. She watched us clean until we had the place looking spick and span.

One of the Sisters had a bunch of keys on a chain that hung from her apron. The keys were for some of the cupboards in the recreation area. We never knew what was in these cupboards, but some were kept locked.

One day, while we were doing our usual Saturday morning cleaning, the Sister decided that we should wash the entire floor in the recreation area. As we gradually washed our way across the floors, we moved whatever furniture there was from one end of the room to the other. Once the entire floor was washed and dried, we got down on our knees and waxed the entire floor. The wax was like a yellowish paste, which came in a five gallon pail. We spread the wax on the floor with a piece of rag.

After that was done, we all got two large mitts, which we used to shine the floor. We knelt down, put our hands in these mitts and rubbed the floor in a circular motion. It was hard work, especially hard on the back.

Then one day after the usual wash and wax, one of the boys had an ingenious idea about shining the floor. He took off his moccasins, pulled the large mitts over his socks and proceeded to shine the floor in a skating fashion. This was much easier than being on our hands and knees shining the floor. After watching him for awhile, we all took off our moccasins or shoes and put the large mitts over our feet. It was a very good idea, but some of the boys got slivers from the wooden floor. After that, we learned to leave our moccasins or shoes on whenever we waxed the floors.

It was during one of these cleaning exercises that I accidentally ran into another boy. He went sprawling across the floor and soon other boys tripped over him. I thought it was a funny sight and I couldn't help laughing.

The Sister saw this and called me over to her side. There were other boys running into each other and fooling around, but for some reason, she picked me out. She called me, and beckoned me to her side with her finger. I expected some scolding as I stood in front of her and stared at the floor.

Suddenly, she grabbed my right hand and took a hold of the two middle fingers. Then she took out her keys and hit me across the top of the hand. It hurt like hell and I cried out. I danced on the spot on my tiptoes, but I didn't dare try to pull my hand away. I was sure that if I had pulled my hand away she would have hit me across the head with her keys. She hit me again and then let go of me.

I just stood there crying and holding my right hand. I looked down and saw a small cut on the top of my right hand, which was bleeding.

Then the Sister told me to wash my hand and waved me away. Still crying, I went to the washroom area and ran some cold water over my hand. Then I stood there, not knowing what to do.

After awhile the Sister came over with a small box. She opened the box and took out a piece of white tape. With her scissors, she cut a narrow strip and placed it over the cut on my hand. It seemed like she had second thoughts and was sorry for what she had done to me, but she didn't apologize. She simply told me that I should behave properly all the time, so I would stay out of trouble. I think this was the only time she ever acted sorry for what she did. She was human after all.

The cut eventually healed, but to this day, I still have that little scar on the top of my right hand as a reminder of that occasion in the residential school.

One day in early fall, the Sister told us that a doctor and a dentist would be visiting the residential school, and each one of us was to be examined by them. The Sister mentioned that we might have to get needles to prevent future sickness and that some of us may have to get our teeth pulled if we had bad teeth.

On the day the plane arrived with the doctor and dentist, we all got ready for the visit. The Sister gave each of us some powdered toothpaste in the palm of our hands. She told us to wet the toothbrush, press it into the powdered stuff and brush our teeth. Up to that time, I couldn't recall ever using any toothpaste; we only used water when we brushed our teeth. Then we all took baths. The Sisters even gave us some clean clothes to wear.

Perhaps the Sister gave us all clean clothes to give the impression to outsiders that this was how we dressed all the time. We also wore our Sunday best for visits from other church dignitaries and special guests, like the school superintendent or Indian Agent. After they left, we went back to wearing our denim coveralls.

We all got in line and nervously waited our turn for a quick examination and possibly a needle. As each boy came out of the doctor's room, he'd say, "Oh, it didn't hurt" or "Didn't feel a thing," forgetting that a few minutes ago, they had been on the verge of crying as they stood in line waiting to see the doctor.

The dentist was a young-looking man and he joked with us as he poked around our teeth. The doctor, on the other hand was serious; he made us cough and poked us with needles in the arm. One of the boys was sitting near a table at the far end of the recreation area. He was crying and mumbling that he must not get a needle. He said his father would scold him and punish him if he got a needle, and that he was forbidden to get needles without his father's permission. I think he was just scared. We watched as he sat crying on the bench. The Sister was standing next to him and telling him to get in line like everyone else.

Finally, she got a hold of him by the arm and dragged him to the door of the doctor's room. The Sister stood with him until it was his turn to see the doctor. When his turn came, the Sister had to push him into the room. A few minutes later, he came out of the doctor's room. He must have felt rather foolish. Sheepishly, he wiped his eyes and half-smiled as he walked by us and went back into the recreation area.

⌖

Sometimes when there was no benediction service in the evening, the Sisters had us say the rosary. This was a prayer devotion consisting of reciting the Hail Mary prayer about five times, each of which began with the Lord's Prayer and ended with the Glory Be To God prayer. There were times when the Sister would call on one of us to lead the prayer session.

This one particular evening, she called on Henry to lead us in prayer. Henry had come to the residential school either from Fort Rae or Yellowknife. He never did talk much about his family, but once in a while, he would talk about his grandmother, who he said raised him. We all knew that Henry stuttered when he spoke, especially when pronouncing certain words, but the stuttering wasn't that bad. Sometimes it didn't require a great deal of effort on his part to speak normally for a few minutes before he would stutter again. However, that night when Henry closed his eyes and opened his mouth to begin the Lord's Prayer, the words wouldn't come out. All he said was, "ah-ah-ah."

We were all kneeling on the floor in our usual places. Most of us had our heads bowed down with our eyes closed, and others just stared at the floor. It was deathly quiet in the room except for the sound of Henry's "ah-ahs".

At times it seemed like he was right on the verge of saying the first words, but still he just couldn't get started with the prayer. We all waited in anticipation. I felt like slapping him on the back to coax him over that first hurdle so he could get started with the prayer. While all this was going on, the Sister remained standing against the wall with a rosary in her hand. She seemed a little amused by the whole situation, and yet she kept her composure and a stern face.

Suddenly, there were giggles here and there, and short busts of suppressed laughter sneaked out between our lips. The Sister moved immediately away from the wall and called for silence. The silence lasted for a little while, then the giggles and snickering would start again as Henry, still with his eyes closed, desperately tried to begin the Lord's Prayer.

One of the boys, George, couldn't contain himself. He held his hand over his mouth and tried very hard not to laugh. With one hand over his mouth, his head shook up and down as he tried to suppress his laughter. Just then, Henry let out some more "ah-ahs", and George looked down at the floor and laughed.

The Sister looked around the room, and then walked over to where George was kneeling. Suddenly, she grabbed him by the shirt collar and dragged him to the middle of the floor. The look on George's face showed that he did not like being treated this way. He began to struggle a bit, twisting this way and that, but the Sister had a firm hold on his collar. There was some shoving between the two of them, and soon, George and the Sister were having it out. George had the Sister on her knees a few times but she still had a hold of him by the collar. George shook his head from side to side, trying to loosen her grip on him. At times, the action would stop and both would hold still for a few seconds.

We all sat on the benches watching the scuffle. No one moved or knew what to do. Meanwhile, Henry still had his eyes closed and his mouth opened. George was just a young boy of eight or nine years old, and here he was, fighting with the Sister. He'd disappear under the Sister's big, long dress a couple of times, trying to loosen her grip, appearing now and then like a swimmer coming up for air.

Finally, George gave up. The Sister still had a hold of his collar, and angrily looked over at us as if to say that she was the winner and still the authority.

This was the only time I ever saw anyone fight with a Sister and it was quite a sight. George ended up doing some kind of penance for his tussle with the Sister. In the end, Henry never did get to say the Lord's Prayer. We finished the rosary with someone else leading the prayers.

One rainy day, we were all in the building, playing various improvised games while we waited for the rain to stop. One of the Sisters called for our attention and told us that we were going to be entertained by another Sister. We all went to our usual seats on the benches along the wall and waited.

Soon, Sister Gagnon came into the room with a suitcase-style box. She told us the instrument in the box was called a steel guitar. This instrument could be played a particular way to sound like Hawaiian music. I'd never heard of Hawaiian music before and didn't know what it sounded like.

The Sister set up the instrument and proceeded to play some tunes for us. It sounded pretty good, but I wasn't familiar with any of the tunes she played. Some of the music she played sounded a little like the back-up steel guitar music we heard on Hank Williams' records at that time.

After she had finished her impromptu concert, we were allowed to view her guitar. Some of us were even allowed to pluck at the strings and use the guitar's slider; it just made noises and no recognizable tune. It certainly was a novelty and a nice change from our daily routine.

A few weeks later, another Sister came into our recreation area with a violin. The Sister said that the instrument was like a Stradivarius, whatever that was; we didn't know at that time. She told us there were only about four or five of these Stradivarius violins left in the entire world. The man who made these instruments had died without leaving any information about how they were made. This time, we were not allowed to touch the instrument, as there were only four or five of them left in the whole world and she certainly didn't want to make it three or four.

The Sister played some fairly slow music for us on the violin. It certainly didn't make you want to get up and dance. We all sat at our usual places and politely listened. I did recognize Ave Maria when she played that tune but the others I had never heard before. Whatever the music, it sure didn't sound anything like Don Messer and his Islanders.

One day, the Sisters gathered all of us in the dining area; this included all the girls. We didn't know what was about to happen. We all sat on our benches at the tables and waited in anticipation. We were told that Sister Gagnon was going to demonstrate a new machine. In a little while, she came down the stairs and entered the dining area. She was carrying a box, which she set on the table that separated the boys and girls.

She opened the box and took out what looked like a record player and placed it on the table. Then as she took the cover off, she said that this machine was called a tape-recorder. It was some new invention. She went on to explain that you could talk into the microphone, which she held in her hand, and the machine would record your voice. Then you could play it back and listen to your own voice. She said it was just like a record player and proceeded to demonstrate.

Some of the boys at the back table stood up on the benches to watch and listen. She placed a short stand on the table and set the microphone on it. Next, she turned on the machine and spoke into the microphone, reading a few lines from a book, then stopped the machine and rewound the tape. We listened as she played it back, and were amazed that it was her voice we actually heard coming out of that machine!

Then the Sister asked for some volunteers, and everyone had their hands up, shouting, "Me, Sister, me!" The Sister looked around and pointed to a young girl. She came forward, looking kind of shy, and stood quietly by the microphone. She looked up at the Sister and it seemed like she really didn't know what to say. Then the Sister asked her to tell a story or sing a song.

The young girl moved closer to the microphone, and after

a little hesitation, she began to sing. It wasn't a religious song or a hymn that we were accustomed to singing. We all waited for the Sister's reaction to the song, and to our surprise, she did nothing. She stood by the mike and coaxed the little girl to continue singing. The girl sang for a while and then her voice sort of faded away. She stopped singing and walked back to her seat.

We all listened to the playback of her song and it sounded pretty good. We smiled and giggled at the novelty of it all. The little girl had broken the ice, and it was all right to sing any kind of song. Soon, a group of us stood in line and waited for our turn to sing or talk into the microphone. Some nervously talked about what they were going to say or sing.

A young boy ahead of us in line was smiling as he looked around like he knew what to do. When his turn came, he stood by the microphone, cleared his throat and in a loud voice said, "I go to school here and I am in grade four." Some of the boys and girls laughed as the boy quickly walked away and sat down.

When my turn came, I was pretty nervous about the whole thing. I had been thinking about what to say or sing. I remembered a Hank Williams' song that I had heard quite often the summer before. I'd heard it enough times to re-member some of the words to the song. It was called *Lonesome Whistle Blowing*, or something like that.

I stood by the microphone and started singing, "*I must ride the number nine . . .*" I sang whatever I could remember of the song. When I was done, I quickly walked back to my bench as the Sister began to rewind the tape. Then we listened to the playback, and it sounded all right.

Years later, I would be in a recording studio, standing in front of two microphones and remembering vividly my first experience with the tape recorder at the residential school. I didn't know it back then, of course, that one day I would actually record a 45 rpm record. The experience with the recording machine at the residential school did not inspire me to pursue a singing career; it never crossed my mind back then. It was just an experience that happened once, and that was that. The residential school system did not prepare you for any kind of a career.

After this first experience with the tape recorder, I often sang for the Sisters who supervised the boys. Sometimes I sang for Father or Sister Superior when they made their unannounced visits to the boys' recreation area. Sister would call me over and tell me to sing. I was put on the spot and there were times I couldn't remember any songs.

One day, the Sister got a guitar, which she brought into the recreation area. We took turns trying to play the guitar but no one knew any chords, nor was there anyone around who knew how to tune a guitar. Eventually, one of the boys learned some chords, and sometimes the Sister had him accompany me on the guitar when I sang for Father or Sister Superior.

We used to practice whenever the chords he knew fit the particular song I was to sing. Then we practiced the same song over and over again. There were times when he accompanied me even if the chords didn't fit the song because they were the only chords he knew how to play, so then it sounded like I was singing off-key.

It took some time, but I was able to learn some guitar chords by watching him. Then during the summer when I had the chance, I'd go to the local square dances and watch others play the guitar, so I learned more chords that way.

Eventually, I learned how to play the guitar and much later on, I even bought one. However, I never did learn how to read music and I still don't. To this day I just play by ear.

⌒

The mission grew a few vegetables: carrots, cabbage, lettuce, tomatoes, corn, and lots of potatoes. There were two large fields where potatoes were planted in the spring and harvested in the fall. The planting took place just before we went home for the summer holidays, and the harvesting took place after we returned to the residential school in the fall. I guess you might say we were cheap labour for the mission.

During the winter months, manure from the barn was dumped onto the snow in the potato fields. Then in early spring, once all the snow was gone, the fields were plowed with horses driven by the Brothers.

The Sisters would give us empty five-gallon pails to collect rocks from the freshly plowed fields. We would dump the rocks into a gully on the ravine by a large log building that was used as a warehouse.

Over time, the gully filled up with the rocks we collected from the two potato fields. It seemed like the rocks grew with the potatoes, because every spring we collected more rocks, which we dumped into the gully. At harvest time, we'd collect more again, and dump those into the gully. To this day, the same gully is still there, although the old log warehouse has long been demolished. The gully is still filled with the rocks, a monument to our hard labour and time spent at the residential school.

While some of us were picking rocks, others were helping the Brothers prepare the potatoes for planting.

The Brothers kept the potatoes in root cellars underneath the priests' residence and the workshop building. The Brothers showed us how to cut the potatoes in half and place them in a gunnysack. We would cut until the designated potato pile was finished, then we'd take all the gunnysacks full of cut potatoes outside to a wagon beside the building. Later, one of the Brothers would take the loaded wagon to the potato fields.

On planting day, we'd go to the fields and watch as one of the Brothers guided the horse-drawn plough across the field. The ground was plowed in straight, narrow trenches the full length of the field. I had never planted potatoes before, so this was going to be a first experience for me. The Brothers showed us how to plant the potatoes. Then they gave us the same pails we used to collect rocks, but this time they were filled with the cut potatoes.

Two of us were assigned to one pail. A five-gallon pail full of potatoes was pretty heavy for us young boys, so we paired up and were able to carry the pail to the end of the trench to start planting. We placed the first potato in the trench cut-side down, just like the way the Brothers showed us. Then we'd place our heel in front of the cut potato and plant another one at the toe of our shoe, continuing this process until we reached the end of the plowed trench or until we ran out of potatoes. Once all the potatoes were planted, the Brothers would plow the trenches over with more dirt.

We had a break once in the morning and again in the afternoon, when the Sisters came out with buns and some water or juice. We would usually walk back to the residential school for lunch, but sometimes we had our lunch out by the fields. Once the planting was completed, we'd all stand around and say a prayer for a good crop. A few days after the planting was done, we would be free again for summer holidays, returning in the fall to pick the potatoes we had planted.

Hauling and piling firewood in the winter

Introduction to skis

Sacred Heart School

CHAPTER FOURTEEN

Back with my family for the summer, our traditional life resumed. This particular summer, my dad and another man got a job cutting firewood for the Hudson's Bay. My sister was away with my uncle's family at their camp downriver, so I stayed with my grandparents in the settlement while my dad was gone. I spent my days fishing, hunting or swimming with the other boys whose families also stayed in the settlement for part of the summer.

Then one day, my dad and his friend arrived in the settlement with a load of firewood. They had built a large raft that held about two or three cords of wood. A canoe was tied to the raft. The two of them sat in the canoe and floated the raft downriver. When the raft drifted too close to the shore or too close to some rocks, one of the men would get on the raft and push it away with a long pole.

We watched the raft for some time as it floated past the RCMP dock. As they approached, the men floated the raft as close to the shore as possible below the Hudson's Bay store. Then both men jumped off, holding onto a long rope, which they quickly tied around a large rock. The raft stopped moving and the current pushed it onshore.

The men then unloaded the raft, piling all the wood onshore. They also dismantled the raft frame, as it, too, could be used for firewood. Next, the hard work of hauling the wood up the riverbank began. It took the men all afternoon and into the evening to haul all the wood up the riverbank and pile it by the Bay manager's house. My dad came home and, needless to say, he was pretty tired. He said they would rest up for a couple of days before going back to cut more firewood.

The next day, a couple of my friends came over and we decided to go fishing below the Hudson's Bay store. We took our fishing lines and hooks, and headed to the riverbank. Just below the store, there were all kinds of empty tin cans, pop bottles and other debris that had come from the store and the manager's house.

The other boys went down the bank as I stopped to tuck my pant legs into my gumboots. I started down the bank but all of a sudden, I tripped. My fishing line and hook went flying in one direction as I tumbled down the bank in another.

I tried to cover my face with my hands as I landed head first into some cans and debris. I fell on top of a large tin can that stuck into my right wrist and into part of my left palm. The other boys came running over to pull the can off my hand. There was blood all over, and I was screaming and crying as the cut began to ache.

One of the boys wrapped my left hand in someone's T-shirt and took me home. My dad took one look at the cut and immediately took me to the clinic at the residential school. By that time, my left hand had stopped bleeding and the shirtsleeve on my right arm had dried over the cut on my wrist. My dad thought I had only cut my left hand. When we got to the clinic, the Sister cleaned the cut on my left hand and bandaged it up.

She gave my dad an extra piece of bandage, in case the cut bled through the one on my hand. I never showed her, nor told her, about the cut on my right wrist, as I really didn't want to go through the pain of getting the sleeve off the cut wrist. I went home like that.

That night, I slept with my shirt on, but while I moved around during the night, the sleeve came off the cut and my wrist bled again. I didn't realize it until the next morning, when my dad woke me up and wanted to know if my left hand was bleeding. There was blood on the shirtsleeve and on the pillow. I started to cry, and told him about the cut on my wrist. He wrapped my wrist with the extra bandage the Sister had given him and said we would have to go back to the clinic. I cried again, knowing that the Sister would put iodine on the cut and it would hurt like hell. I followed my dad to the clinic again. The Sister was nice about the whole thing. She told me I should have shown her the cut on my wrist, as she would have bandaged it up properly so it wouldn't bleed.

It could have been dangerous. The cut on my wrist could have caused a lot of blood loss. The Sister never offered to stitch up the cuts; I don't think the clinic was equipped for something like that. For the better part of the summer, I had my hand and wrist bandaged up. Eventually, they both healed over. Today I have the scars, a reminder of my childhood experience of falling into the garbage and debris below the old Bay store.

When we weren't fishing or swimming, and we didn't have anything else to do, we'd go to the local dump and look for an old inner tube of a truck tire. If we were lucky enough to find one, we'd make sling-shots. Then we'd go off into the bushes with our pockets full of small rocks, which we'd use to shoot at grouse, rabbits and other such small game.

On returning from one of these hunting excursions with my friends, Tom and Fred, we walked by one of the potato fields. The potato leaves were fairly tall and some had small, white flowers on the branches. We went through the barbed wire fence and into the potato field. Then we dug around one plant and found some potatoes. Eventually, we dug around at random and collected a bunch of potatoes.

We sat down and proceeded to peel a few. At first we nibbled at them, just to find out what they tasted like. They weren't too bad so we ate a couple of them. We also dug up a few carrots and ate those, too. We took what we had left and went home, thinking nothing would result from this episode.

The next afternoon, I was with Tom, sitting in the shade behind his parent's tent, when the local RCMP officer arrived and asked for us by name. We got up and moved to the front of the tent. The officer asked us if we knew anything about what had happened in the mission potato field. Naturally, we replied no. He then said we were not telling him the truth, as Fred already told him the story and had given him our names.

Apparently, one of the brothers found a few potato plants had been pulled out while he was pulling weeds. When he was out for his usual bicycle ride later that evening, he happened to see one of the RCMP officers and stopped for some casual conversation. He mentioned the incident to the officer.

The following day, the officer walked among the tents, asking if anyone knew anything about the incident in the mission potato field. As luck would have it, he happened to walk by Fred's parents' tent while Fred was by the fireplace boiling up some potatoes. Now, back in those days, we didn't buy potatoes from the stores like we do nowadays. The only place to buy potatoes was from the mission. The officer knew right then that he had his man. When confronted, Fred told him about the episode and gave him our names.

The officer told us to go with him. I was scared and thought that he would take us to jail. It was a relief when, instead, he took us to the mission. There, the priest gave us a talk about behaviour, and for our penance, he said we would have to weed the two potato fields for one whole day.

Early the next day, we arrived at the mission and the priest told us to see the brothers in the workshop. The door to the shop was open, so we stood in the doorway and watched them working on something. Then one of them noticed us, came outside, and pointed to the shovels and the two wheelbarrows next to the building. He waved us over with his arm and we followed him to the furthest field.

There, he showed us what to do and what kinds of plants to pull out. He told us to make sure we didn't pull out any of the potato plants. We weeded all that morning and threw the weeds into the wheelbarrow. Once it was full, we took it down to the ravine where we had dumped the rocks earlier in the spring. We kept this up until the Brother came for us at lunchtime. We ate in the dining room used by the hired help. I didn't think we needed supervision during our lunch, but one of the Brothers ate with us. He said grace before and after our meal. After lunch, we continued weeding.

It was late afternoon and we were just about done with the first field. There was still another field to be weeded. We continued pulling weeds until one of the Brothers came and took us back to the mission. Our hands were hurting, as we didn't have any gloves. The priest asked if we had learned our lesson after a long, hot day of weeding in the field. Naturally, we said yes. Then he said he would pay us if we would come back the next day to finish weeding the potato fields. Again, naturally, we said yes.

We showed up at the mission bright and early the next day. We were eager to work, as we would be paid when we finished the job. We went directly to the shop where the Brother gave us the shovels and wheelbarrows again. We finished weeding the first field and walked down the ravine to the other one. This field was smaller than the first, so we were done weeding early that afternoon.

I had told the other boys that maybe the Father would pay us five dollars each for the day. We could buy some .22 shells and go hunting at the mission prairie, or go someplace downriver. Or we could buy some gas for the kicker and go fishing at the creek across the river. We had already planned how to spend our anticipated five dollars pay.

Eagerly, we returned the wheelbarrows and the shovels to the workshop and walked to the mission, anticipating a good day's pay. To our surprise, the Father paid us each two dollars for the day's work. Immediately I remembered my dad had once told me that he had worked at cutting hay for the mission for two dollars a day. Tom, Fred and I looked at each other and didn't say anything.

Then the Father said he would open the mission store if we wanted to buy some candies. Again we looked at each other and shrugged our shoulders, declining the offer. We were a little afraid because no one ever said no to a priest. To our surprise, the Father shrugged his shoulders and said nothing. Tom, Fred and I went home, free to spend the two dollars on whatever we wanted.

Some days, the Sisters would let us visit our rabbit snares after school, when we didn't have to bring in the firewood, and sometimes, on Saturday mornings, the Sister would let us leave early after breakfast to check our snares and traps. Once, Tom, Fred and I skinned a rabbit that wasn't completely frozen and cooked it over a fire we had made along riverbank on the other side of the Mission Island. That way, no one from the residential school or the mission could see the smoke from our fire. Cooking a rabbit over the fire was nothing new to us. It sure tasted good and it was just like being back home in the bush.

Later on, before we got back onto the ice on the Snye, we rolled around in the snow and rubbed each other's outer clothing with small spruce boughs. Then we rolled around again in the snow. We did this to get rid of the smell of the smoke from our clothing. It must have worked, because no one seemed to notice; if they did, they never said anything.

One Saturday morning after breakfast, we were allowed to go out into the bush to visit our rabbit snares. On this occasion the same two boys went with me to check our snares. When we got to the place we called One Mile, we decided to hike overland on the dog team trail to the other side of the island. From One Mile, the trail went across the Snye, up the bank into the bush over the island, and followed the river to Lishamie and other villages further downriver. When we arrived at the Mackenzie River, we decided to go on and visit my grandparents.

Lishamie was only about three miles or so away down the river from where we stood on the trail, and we had already covered close to two miles. We followed the dog team trail, which was packed with hard snow from constant travel. This made for easy walking without sinking into the snow. We kept up a steady pace, running at times.

We were like the "three amigos." We had got ourselves into trouble pulling out potatoes in the mission fields. Now here we were, Tom, Fred and me, running down the trail to a place we were not allowed to go to.

We arrived at the mouth of the channel and kept on going. As the trail rounded a bend in the channel, we saw the first log house. Grandfather's house was the last one at the end of the channel. The main trail ran along the shore, with side trails going up the riverbank to each of the houses.

We continued on until we came to a fork on the trail that led up the riverbank to Grandfather's house. We walked up the riverbank and went into the house. Grandfather looked up from what he was doing and asked if I had run away from the residential school again. We all laughed, and I told him we just wanted to know if we could make it here and back in one day.

No one from the village came around to ask why we were there. Grandfather said most of the men were away on their traplines; that's why there was no activity around the village. A little while later, Grandmother gave us some bannock and hot tea.

We enjoyed this snack, but our visit had to be short and soon we were on our way back.

We kept up a steady pace like we had done on our way down, and ran once in a while. We were trying to get back before everyone was called in for supper. It was wintertime, so it got dark fairly early. We got to the trail leading overland to One Mile and kept right on going. There was a pale moon overhead and we could make out the outline of the trail in the dim light.

We got to One Mile and carried on across the Snye in the direction of the Girls' Shack, then made our way across the field to the barn. To our relief, some of the boys were still playing outside when we passed the barn and entered the boys' yard. A short time later, the Sister blew her whistle for the boys to come in for supper.

We never mentioned to anyone that we had gone to Lishamie. I imagine we would have been in big trouble if any of the Sisters knew, because we were not allowed to go far away from the designated residential school area. No one expected any of us to run home and come back to residential school in one day, but we did.

∽

It was early one spring day when my dad and my brother, Daniel, came to visit Josie and me at the residential school. My dad told us then that Grandmother had passed away. Grandfather was now on his own, but one of my brothers would live with him and look after him.

At the end of June, we left the residential school again for the summer. Once again, the field behind the Bay compound was filled with tents. Most of the people had arrived to take their children out of the residential school and stay for the annual treaty payment and celebrations. It was also a time for re-acquaintances and renewed friendships.

Grandfather's tent was among those behind the Bay compound. We had our tent further back. The men still came around, especially in the evenings, to listen to Grandfather's stories. They would all sit on the grass in a semi-circle at the opening of the tent. When it got too warm inside, the men would raise the flaps all around to allow some breeze into the tent. Some of us brought up water or tea for the men.

Then one day, Grandfather fell sick. It may have been pneumonia, or possibly just old age. He lay propped up with some blankets in his tent. He spoke in a low voice, sometimes almost a whisper. He looked frail and was not like the man I remembered at Lishamie. Then, he was usually busy around his house or he was off in the bush setting or checking his rabbit snares.

I recalled a time a few years earlier, when Grandfather had wanted to build a bear trap. Fresh bear meat would be good, especially an animal fattened on berries. Back then, there were no tin cans, plastic bags and other containers scattered all over the place. At that time, bears just ate fish and berries.

Grandfather decided to build the bear trap across the river in a stand of large spruce trees where there were plenty of cranberries. When we got to the area, I sat on a log and watched as Grandfather pointed to a spot by some large spruce trees and asked a couple of the men to cut two large logs.

Then he cut some dried poles that he set up like a small teepee. We helped him cover this with aspen branches, moss and spruce boughs. The bait—a whole fish—was put into a piece of gunnysack. A length of rope was tied to the gunnysack, which was hung in the middle of the small teepee.

Meanwhile, the men had cut the two logs and dragged them over to the spot. One was placed on the ground in between two standing spruce trees. With some difficulty, the men placed the other heavy log at an angle over the first one. A short pole, about four feet in length, was placed between the two logs, and the rope from the bait was then tied to this short pole.

The idea was for that the animal to enter the trap by stepping over the log on the ground. In doing so, its body would be positioned over this log, with both front and hind legs on either side. Once the animal grabbed the bait and pulled on the line, the pole would give way, causing the other log to fall full weight on the animal, breaking its back and killing it.

I remember on the morning we were to check the bear trap, the wind had come up and created big waves on the river. So the next day we went to the trap site. A couple of the men went ahead with guns and we followed behind. As we approached the trap, one of them yelled that there was something in it. He wasn't quite sure if it was dead, so he shot at the animal with a 30-30 rifle. It turned out to be a large black bear. The log had landed on its back and killed it. It looked big and bloated.

Grandfather then asked the men to skin the bear. Among the Dene, there is an overall principle of respect for animals. This respect came from the Dene's understanding of the importance of the animals, which they depended on for survival. The Dene took care to see to the proper disposal of the meat, leaving parts for the other animals to eat. Grandfather didn't reset the trap and we went back to our camp.

This was what I remembered of Grandfather, and now here he was, a very sick man. At that time, the thought of him dying never crossed my mind. I only knew he was very sick. There were some men by his side in the tent and other men and women outside. The priest was also there, having given him the last rites. Sometime later, the priest announced that Grandfather had passed away. There was a long pause of silence, interrupted by a few sobs among those present. The men closed the tent laps and sat on the ground with the others.

Although Grandfather was not my biological grandfather, I respected and loved him as though he had been. I was sad to see him go, although later I would celebrate his life by being happy that he had been my grandfather, that he had come from Lishamie, and that I had heard his stories.

He once said, "After the missionaries came, things began to slow down." This is the literal translation of what he said in our language. What he had probably meant was that the practice of our traditional ceremonies was beginning to decline, along with the use of our language. His words were prophetic because we are continuing to experience exactly that today, long after his passing. He lived at a time that marked the beginning of the difficult transitional years for the Dene people.

∽

One summer day, two young men arrived in Fort Providence on the Bishop's plane. They would be the new teachers at the residential school, and this would be my second experience with non-religious order teachers, meaning they weren't priests, Brothers or Sisters.

My first experience had been during my third year at the residential school. We didn't see too much of that teacher; he kept mostly to himself in the residential school building and in his renovated room, and rarely played any kind of sports with us after school. He socialized more with the Bay manager, the members of the Royal Signal Corps, and the RCMP. This would be the norm with future teachers, new Bay managers, nurses and RCMP officers who came to our community. They would socialize amongst each other or with other non-native people in the community, rarely with the local people. I think it was partly because they couldn't relate to the Dene people or their way of life. This division likely still happens today in some northern communities.

Somehow, I had a different feeling about the new teachers. They were curious and asked questions about the settlement and about what people did in their camps. They seemed to want to acquaint themselves with their new surroundings. Some days, we would see them fishing along the shore below the Hudson's Bay store. We never formally met them until we were back in the residential school. One teacher was named Ron and the other was Walter. We never did call them by their first names. Everyone called them "Teacher." It didn't matter if you were talking to Ron or Walter — it was always "Teacher."

Besides teaching, the two men set about trying to introduce us to new things, things the Sisters didn't have or, perhaps, didn't want us to have. They bought an electric record player and some long playing records. This was our first introduction to the record album. Back home, we were used to the old thick '78' records and the old gramophone that you had to wind up to operate. The new machine was plugged into the wall outlet and we listened to the music.

They also ordered some real movies. Previously, all we had ever seen were some of the National Film Board movies, which were mostly documentary-style films. We also had seen some cartoons from the National Film Board. Very few of us had ever seen a full-length feature movie.

My first feature movie experience was a western the new teachers had ordered, called *Taza, Son of Cochise* or some similar title. Years later, when I was at the university, I was in the library gathering some information for a paper when I found some material on Cochise. Curious, I read a couple pages of the material. It turned out that Cochise, indeed, had an older son named Taza, who later became chief of the Chiricahua Apaches after Cochise died. How historically factual that movie was, I don't know, but it was a big change from the usual National Film Board films. The star in this movie could have been Rock Hudson or some other actor who looked like him. The movie was about the usual fight between the American Cavalry and the Indians.

This particular movie was shown in the residential school dining area, and the people from the settlement were invited to attend. A few women were sitting on the bench across from us. They were all curiously watching the movie when, suddenly, one of them said in South Slavey, "Those Indians look like white men." We weren't aware then, but she was probably right about the Hollywood Indians in the movie.

To many of us who were watching a movie like this for the first time, it was quite something, especially the action. In the battle scenes, we saw people falling off cliffs and getting shot with bullets and arrows. Some people were getting stabbed with knives and lances. It looked very real, and it was sometimes frightening. A few times, I put my head down during a fight scene if someone was about to get stabbed. I think it scared some of the other boys too.

For days after that, we talked about nothing but the movie. We even started playing cowboys and Indians, which we'd never done before. Of course, no one wanted to play the part of the Indians — they seemed to lose all the time.

Being young, we never considered ourselves "Indians" like the ones we'd see in comic books or movies. We didn't wear loincloths like the Indians in the movies. These were Indians who lived down south on the prairies in the States; they were not like us. We were Dene people. But eventually, as we grew older, we learned otherwise.

In the fall when the Snye froze over, we went skating with the new teachers. They taught us how to play real hockey. One team would wear armbands so we could tell who our teammates and opponents were. They showed us how to make plays by passing the puck to our team members. It was more like a thinking game, where you tried to outwit your opponent, rather than just knock them over and steal the puck.

The teachers showed us how to place ourselves: in the centre, on the left and right wings, and on the left and right defense positions. Before this, we used to play by taking the puck away from another boy and skating with it the full length of the ice to put it into the net. Everyone was for himself and all over the ice. The teachers taught us how to play an organized hockey game based on teamwork.

The new teachers also introduced us to the Boy Scouts, and most of us joined up. They explained what a Boy Scout was all about and how to win merit badges for doing good deeds. We made staves from tall, narrow spruce or tamarack trees. Some of us even carved symbols on the staves. The teachers even ordered Boy Scouts' uniforms for us, which I believe they purchased with their own money. We made bone rings for the scarves we wore with our uniform. Our Boy Scout activities were a lot of fun, and a big change from the usual routine of the residential school.

Early in the spring, after the ice had melted, the teachers took us fishing. The Snye, which was usually low and dry in some places, was now flooded. Water was running its full length and emptying into the Mackenzie River a few miles downstream.

We walked towards the Girls' Shack and watched as the teachers fished for awhile along the shore of the Snye. They weren't catching anything so we all walked along to the place we called One Mile, continued on the road towards Bluefish Creek, and followed a trail that led to the bank of the Snye and into a clearing.

The teachers cast their lines out again as some of us played around in the bush along the shore. We took turns and tried our luck at fishing. For some of us, it was the first time we had ever used a rod and reel. The teachers showed us how to cast and reel in the line and hook. We fished the rest of the morning and into the afternoon without any luck. We had a fire going, just in case somebody caught a fish. By late afternoon, we were all getting pretty hungry, as we hadn't had anything to eat since breakfast that morning.

One of the teachers picked up his packsack and sat by the fire. He opened the bag and took out a loaf of bread and a couple of cans of beans. The other teacher opened the cans with a hunting knife and we made bean sandwiches, which I thought then were the best sandwiches I had ever eaten. Some of us toasted our bread over the fire and had toasted bean sandwiches. After we had our fill of bean sandwiches, we prepared to make our way back to the residential school.

We followed the same trail along the riverbank taking, our time, stopping here and there. We arrived late into the evening so the teachers invited us to spend the night at their house. One of them said he would talk to the Sister the next day. Although we hadn't caught any fish, it sure was nice just to get away from the residential school, even for one day.

I mentioned the fishing trip to my dad when he came to visit us at the residential school. He told me at that time of the year when the water was high, the fish, especially the pikes, would come into the tall grass and weeds along the shore to spawn. When that would happen, the fish wouldn't eat as much; maybe that was why we hadn't caught any fish.

One day, the teachers came into our recreation room just as one of the Sisters was giving the boys their usual haircuts. After awhile, one of the teachers offered to cut the boy's hair, and the Sister politely gave him the clippers.

The teacher cut a little bit of hair and combed it back. Then he stepped to the front to look at the boy before cutting his hair again. He styled the boy's hair in a fashion that was totally unlike the haircuts we got from the Sister. The Sister usually placed the clipper on our necks and cut the hair straight up, all around the base of our heads. Before long, most of us got in line for a haircut from the teacher.

The teacher gave a couple of boys a haircut style he called the brush-cut. He said we wouldn't have to comb our hair with this kind of a haircut. A few of us then asked for the brush-cut, until some of the other boys began teasing each other, calling the brush-cut boy a "monkey-head." So naturally, the next time around, the boy wouldn't want another brush-cut.

The new teachers ordered more movies, which they showed to the people from the settlement. Sometimes, they would charge a dollar or fifty cents to see the movies. The movies were free if they were repeat showings. Some were religious-type movies, like the one about Saint Bernadette or about the three children from Fatima who claimed to have seen the Virgin Mary.

For many of the local people, they were the first feature-length movies they ever saw, and they watched the films, almost mesmerized by the actions and special effects. Some of them even wondered how the film-makers ever managed to take pictures of the Virgin Mary. The priest tried to explain that it was all acting and make-believe with film tricks. He probably wished that he could attract that same kind of enthusiasm from the people with his Sunday sermons.

FROM LISHAMIE

CHAPTER FIFTEEN

When the school year ended, the new teachers decided to go back south for their holidays and visit their families for part of the summer. One of them, Ron, asked Father Superior if it was possible for one of the boys to go with him and experience farm life for the summer. When the Father asked me, I readily accepted, but he said that I would have to ask for my dad's permission.

When my dad came to visit me at the residential school, I told him about the possible trip down south. I would travel with one of the teachers to his parents' farm. My dad took me with him to talk to Father Superior and ask for advice. The Father suggested talking to the teacher, so I followed them as they walked to the teachers' house and I waited outside while the Father took my dad into the house to talk to the teachers.

After some time, they came out and my dad reluctantly gave his permission for me to go south for the summer. The condition was that when I returned, I would stay with him for at least a week before I went back to the residential school in the fall. I was surprised that the Father agreed to this condition. He said that I would most likely be home sometime around the middle of August.

My dad told me that I was to behave at all times and that he wouldn't be around to help if I got into any trouble. Naturally, like any other boy, I promised to be good and listen to whoever was looking after me. I wouldn't be going home like the other boys this summer, but I was going to a different place to experience new things.

Having grown up in Lishamie and Fort Providence, I had never been anywhere else. I waited in anticipation for the Bishop's plane to arrive and take us away on the first leg of our journey south. The trip would definitely give me the opportunity to experience many things for the first time in my life.

When the plane arrived, the Bishop stayed on for a couple of days. He celebrated mass in the big church and performed the confirmation ceremony. Some of the boys and girls also received their first communion. The church was crowded with people; most of them had arrived to take their children out of the residential school for the summer.

A couple of days later, Ron came over to inform the Sister and me that we would be leaving the next day. The Sister gave me a suitcase and all my clean clothes. She also gave me a couple pairs of new socks and a couple of new shirts, which I packed in the suitcase along with my other belongings.

The next afternoon, Ron, Walter and I walked down to the mission dock where the Bishop's plane was tied up. There were many people standing around on the riverbank by the priests' residence, waiting to watch the Bishop's departure.

The Brother put the suitcases and bags into the plane as we waited onshore. At last, the Bishop made his way down with his pilot and another Brother. As was his habit, the Bishop stopped here and there, talking to some of the local people who had come to watch him leave. Finally, he came on board and the plane slowly taxied out onto the river for take-off.

The noise of the plane grew louder as it picked up speed. I looked out the window and watched the water splash against the pontoon as the plane lifted out of the water. Then it seemed like the plane was riding on top of the water, and soon we were in the air.

The pilot made a circle over the settlement, as was the custom, a sort of goodbye gesture. The settlement looked small from up in the sky. I looked down and tried to recognize some of the houses and tents as the plane levelled off and away we flew towards Hay River. As we flew, I looked out over the lake and land, trying to recognize some familiar places. We flew over Big Island and on past Wrigley Harbor where the barges tied up before travelling across the big lake or down the Mackenzie River.

After a thirty-minute flight, I could feel the plane descend to land on the Hay River. Again, the plane rode the water for a while and slowed right down. Then the pilot taxied to a large, wooden dock and the Brother got out to tie up the plane. We got out and waited for the Brother to unload our baggage. I looked around and saw part of the Indian Village across the river. There were a few canoes along the shore just below the big church, which looked almost like the one back home. The church was the most visible building, as it sat close to the edge of the riverbank.

We said goodbye to the Bishop and thanked him for the plane ride. Then, carrying our bags, we walked to town, following a trail through the bush. Back then, Hay River consisted of what is now the old town and a few houses in the West Channel. We walked down the trail until we came upon a partial sidewalk, then we followed the sidewalk up to a building where we were to catch the bus. Ron bought our tickets and checked-in our baggage.

Ron asked if I wanted something to eat and pointed to a building down the street. I nodded and followed him to the coffee shop. We sat down by a window and he ordered us some sandwiches and drinks. I had a fried egg sandwich and an Orange Crush to drink. This was my very my first restaurant experience.

Later, we walked to the Hudson's Bay store, stopping for a while at the pool hall to kill some time before heading back to the coffee shop. The teachers had coffee and I had another Orange Crush. From here, Walter would stay overnight and catch the flight to Edmonton the next afternoon. We said our goodbyes and went back to where the bus was parked. We waited a while before the driver motioned us to get on the bus. A few moments later, we were on our way, and this was the beginning of my first bus ride. The narrow, gravel highway seemed to follow the riverbank for some distance.

The first stop was Indian Cabins, where some of the passengers had a meal in the coffee shop. There were some Indians talking outside the coffee shop before getting on the bus, and I could understand their conversation. I found out much later that these people had been Slavey Dene, just like me. The bus stopped once in awhile to let some of them got off. They must have had camps along the river.

When we arrived at Meander River, the bus pulled up to the Hudson's Bay building with its familiar white walls and red roof. There were some more Indian people getting off and on the bus. They also spoke Slavey, but a few spoke too fast for me to understand. The bus driver loaded up a bag of mail and boxes of groceries that a few passengers had bought from the store. Soon we were on our way again. I slept in short intervals, waking up whenever the bus stopped to let people off with their supplies or to let new passengers on.

At High Level, the bus pulled up alongside a hotel. The driver announced that we would be at this stop for awhile, so we could have a meal or walk around. We all got off and the driver drove the bus away. I thought the bus was leaving us behind, but Ron told me that the driver had to unload the mail and other things, and then reload more mail and supplies for other towns along the way.

We went into the restaurant and sat down at a booth by the window. The interior of the restaurant seemed large, with booths along one wall and stools along the counter. I let Ron order us a meal, as I was not familiar with the food listed on the menu. After we finished our meal, we walked around close to the hotel until it was time for us to go.

It seemed like the bus stopped at every small place or farm along the way. At Peace River, the bus stopped alongside a building with a restaurant nearby, where we had another meal. Again, we had time to walk around for awhile. It was my first time in a large town, and I noticed there were many houses, all different sizes, shapes, colours and heights. The houses reminded me of the pictures in the Dick and Jane books back at the residential school. There were also many vehicles, more than I had ever seen before.

Beyond Peace River, part of the highway was paved so the bus ride was fairly smooth. We travelled through the night, stopping here and there at different places. The next morning, I saw many more houses as the bus approached the city.

The bus made its way through several streets, and I could see more houses and some stores. We stopped by a large building where other buses were parked, then got off and waited for our suitcases to be unloaded. After picking up our suitcases, we walked into the bus depot.

There were lockers along the wall of a large room. People were sitting here and there on long benches. Some were reading and others were napping. We put our suitcases into a large locker and went into the café and ordered breakfast.

There was music coming from another booth, like someone was listening to the radio. Ron told me that it wasn't the radio; the music coming from a machine called a jukebox. He said some booths in the café had these machines where you can make a selection from the list of songs, put in a dime or a quarter and listen to the music in your own booth. After we ate, Ron made a phone call and we waited for our ride. Soon, Ron's brother-in-law and nephew came to pick us up at the bus depot. We put our suitcases into the back of the pickup and drove off into the City of Edmonton.

It was my first time in a city and everything looked so big. Tall buildings lined the streets just off the sidewalks. There were lots of stores and lots of people walking around. There were also many vehicles on the road, stopping and going, waiting for the traffic lights to change. It was quite an exciting ride for me to Ron's brother-in-law's house.

We stayed in Edmonton for the next couple of days, mainly to recuperate from the long bus trip. But far from being tired, I was excited about being in a new place. I walked around with Ron's nephew, exploring some stores and taking in the local sights.

Many years later, I would meet Ron's nephew again by chance. He was on a vacation in Yellowknife, and stopped for gas at the local service station. At that time, I was the settlement administrator for Fort Providence and he was a bank manager in Fort McMurray, Alberta. I was sure surprised to see him, and even more surprised that he remembered me after all those years.

While we were in Edmonton, I got a chance to go to the local fast food drive-in; it may have been Burger King or A&W, I don't recall which, but it was my very first time in such a place. Everyone ordered something to eat, but I only ordered a pop. I wasn't familiar with the items on the menu and I didn't want the others to know about it, so I pretended that I wasn't hungry enough to order food.

Hamburger was new to me and I certainly didn't want to eat chicken, which was also new to me. I just didn't know how they were going to serve the chicken. The only chickens I was familiar with were the ones at the residential school, and then there were the spruce grouse and prairie chickens. Once I saw the food that was served, I knew what to order the next time I came to a similar fast food drive-in.

Back home at Fort Providence, we didn't have hamburgers, hot dogs, French fries or any other fast food items when I was growing up. Nowadays, these things are commonplace. Maybe it was a good thing, because today I rarely go to fast food places, I rarely eat potato chips and my favourite drink is iced-tea, not pop.

Soon it was time for us to leave the city and travel to Ron's hometown. Ron's brother-in-law drove us to the train station. We said our goodbyes and gathered up our suitcases. There were many people inside the station, either waiting to leave or waiting to pick up somebody. The station looked very large to me. It had a high ceiling, which reminded me of the church back home, and benches, just like in the bus depot.

When our departure was announced, we walked out with the rest of the passengers and got on the train, taking our seats. Soon, the train got underway and just like my two previous trips on the plane and the bus, this would be my very first train ride. I looked out the window as the train travelled through the city, watching the city lights grow dim as the train pulled further away. Soon there were no lights at all, except for a few from the farmhouses here and there. We were on our way to Wilkie, Saskatchewan, where Ron's parents lived on a farm.

One of Ron's brothers, Fred, came to meet us at the train station and took us to his parents' house in town. Ron's parents were at the farm a few miles out of town. They also had a nice house in town, which Ron's brothers or sister used when they worked in Wilkie. We stayed there that night, and the next day we drove to the farm and met Ron's parents. They were an elderly German couple, and spoke mostly German to each other and to their sons; they spoke English to me and to their grandchildren. At times, they lived on the farm by themselves when their kids had to work in town.

The house was situated in the left corner of a large lot. A mixture of hedges surrounded the whole lot. They grew tall in some places and were kept trimmed at the driveway. Across from the house was a large shed that held some farm equipment. A little ways from the house was the chicken coop, and right next to it was a large barn. There were bails of straw neatly piled against one wall of the barn. Next to the barn was a small shed with a sloping roof and a fenced-in yard for some pigs. Another fenced-in yard close by held a few cows for milking that evening.

On my first day on the farm, we drove around and Ron showed me the huge fields of wheat, alfalfa and barley. Ron said he would show me how to ride a horse, which would be another first for me. That first evening at supper, Ron's father said grace before we all sat down to eat. They said grace again after supper. This was something I was very familiar with because we did this at the residential school.

After supper, I helped Ron's mother clear off the dinner table. Then I sat down in the living room. Everyone was curious, asking Ron about his experiences in the north, especially teaching in Fort Providence. Ron told them a few stories about fishing, camping, canoe trips down the river, and so on.

After awhile, Ron's parents came into the living room. They sat at the table and chatted for a few minutes until Ron's father said something and everyone knelt on the floor. Then he led us in the rosary. They prayed in their own language, which to me was new and fascinating. I had heard prayers in Latin, French, and English, and in my own language, but I'd never heard a prayer in German.

Once the prayers ended, the men talked among themselves for awhile, and then went to bed. To me, it seemed a little too early for bed at that time of the evening, but I learned that these farm people got up with the dawn to put in a good day's work.

I had a wonderful time that summer. I was far away from the residential school and at a place that I had only read about or saw pictures of in the schoolbooks. I thought of my dad and sister once in awhile, but I knew I was going home to see them again. Unlike being at the residential school, I was free to play around, ride a bike, ride a horse and do other things that kept me busy for the better part of the day. I also wasn't restricted or confined within an enclosure on the farm.

At the farm that summer, Ron's dad showed me how to start the tractor by cranking it up. It was similar to the way the Brothers started the old tractor back at the residential school. He even showed me how to drive the tractor, although it was only within the farmyard. I also tried my hand at driving a truck, except I had difficulty starting it. I would turn the key in the ignition but in order for the engine to turn over and start, I had to step on a knob sticking out of the floor of the truck. My leg was too short to reach that far down, but I kept trying until I did manage to get it started. Then I sat next to the old man and steered the truck. He had his foot on the gas pedal because my legs couldn't reach that far down. This was a fun learning time for me.

Sometimes, I went with Ron's mom to the chicken coop, where she showed me how to pick up the eggs. She would simply reach under the chicken and take out an egg or two. Then I would try, but sometimes the chicken would peck at my hands and arms, and I'd quickly pull my hand back. She would laugh, take my hand and gently place it under the chicken and take the egg. I kept trying and eventually I was able to get the eggs on my own.

I went to a lot of movies that summer. These were mostly western movies with cowboys and Indians. I sat in the theater with my friends, who were white boys. It didn't bother them in the least that I was Indian. It didn't bother me, either, that I was Indian or that they were white. At that age, children don't seem to notice differences in race or colour. We were friends, just kids enjoying the movies. The Indians in the movies were American Indians, like the Apache, Cheyenne or Sioux. Audie Murphy and John Wayne would always win the battles against all kinds of odds.

I also went to my first drive-in movie that summer. The cars were all parked in rows in what looked like a field. Up front was a large, white screen. We parked the car next to a short, steel pole with a speaker hanging from it. We took the speaker, placed it inside the car window and listened to the movie, which I think was called *Stagecoach*.

One day, Ron's sister and brother-in-law arrived with their family from Edmonton. They were on their way to a lake to do some fishing, and invited us to go along. After breakfast early the next morning, we left for our fishing trip. We drove on a gravel road for awhile until we reached the paved highway. The scenery along the highway all looked the same to me: fields of wheat and farmhouses here and there. It was some time before we finally arrived at the cabin Ron's brother-in-law had rented on the lakeshore.

It was raining when we arrived, so we didn't go fishing that afternoon or that evening. We stayed at the cabin by the lake for the next couple of days, which turned out to be warm and sunny. It was a good time to be out on the lake. The boat floated lazily on the water, drifting with the light wind that blew from time to time. We shared rods and tried our luck at fishing. I don't remember anyone catching any fish, although we did try every day.

Back on the farm, I took the cows out to pasture every morning and brought them back every evening for milking. Sometimes I'd walk to the pasture to fill two large wooden troughs with water for the cows. The pasture was a large, fenced-in field with a pond that attracted all kinds of ducks. I would walk down to the pond and start the pump to fill the troughs with water. Sometimes, I would ride down to the pasture on a bicycle. It was faster than walking.

One day, Ron's father said they were going to butcher a couple of pigs to take to the market in Battleford. He built a fire and placed a forty-five-gallon barrel on top. Then he filled half of it with water from the garden hose. While waiting for the water to boil, he went into the pigpen and marked two of the pigs on the ears. Meanwhile, I filled the long trough along the fence with a pail of some mixture and the pigs all ran over to feed.

Ron's father sent me back to the house to pick up some knives in a pail that had been left on the porch. A few minutes later, I returned to see them pull the dead pigs out of the pen. I didn't know how they had killed the pigs. I was curious but I didn't ask. I watched as Ron sprayed water over the dead pigs to wash off the mud. Then, Ron's father asked if I wanted to help scrape the hair off the pigs. I never knew pigs had hair; I always thought they only had smooth skin. One of the pigs was hung from a tripod and dunked into the barrel of hot water. As soon as it was out of the water, we used our knives to scrape the hair off the skin. Later, the pigs were butchered, covered in a tarp and hung overnight in the shed.

The next day, we went to Battleford. I saw my first rodeo there; I also saw some other Indians at that rodeo. Many of them wore cowboy hats, cowboy shirts and cowboy boots. They must have been cowboy Indians, I thought. I saw other Indians on horses when I went over to watch some bronco riding and barrel races.

The rodeo was crowded with people. It was just like a big fair, with all kinds of stands for food and games. It was at one of these food stands that I finally had a hamburger, which tasted delicious. It was late evening when we left and we returned to the farm that night.

I never paid much attention to the time or to what day of the week or month it was, until one day, Ron told me that we would be leaving in a few days. Soon we were getting ready to leave the farm. Ron's mother washed my clothes, and once again, I packed my suitcase. We said goodbye to Ron's parents, then his brother, Fred, drove us to the train station. On the way, Ron told me I would be travelling alone after we got to Edmonton, heading by bus back to Hay River. Once in Hay River, I was to go to the priest's house, and my dad would meet me there to take me back home.

We arrived in Edmonton and went directly to the bus depot. We had something to eat at the café, and Ron stayed with me until it was time for me to board the bus. He told me he would most likely visit Fort Providence to see some of the kids because he may be teaching or supervising at the mission school in Fort Resolution that fall. This would depend on the office of the Bishop in Fort Smith.

The return bus trip was uneventful, with stops at the usual places. I slept off and on during the entire bus trip. Once in awhile, when the bus stopped long enough, I would get off to stretch, get some fresh air or to buy a bottle of pop. Somehow, the return trip seemed to take longer than the trip out.

At High Level, some young Indian people got on the bus. They seemed to be students and they were all speaking English, although and I heard some Slavey here and there in their conversation. One girl came over and politely asked me where I was going. I told her I was on my way to Hay River to meet my dad. She told me that she and her friends had come to High Level for some kind of fall celebration, and they were on their way back to Meander River. After we left Meander River, I slept off and on again as the bus bounced down the gravel highway to Hay River.

Finally, after what seemed like many long hours, we arrived at Hay River. Upon getting my suitcase, I asked for directions to the local priest's house and went there directly, as I was told to do. I met the priest and he told me that my dad had left earlier to meet the bus. I must have missed him as I rushed to get to the priest's house. I left my suitcase there and walked back to the bus depot. I found my dad standing by the building, looking around for me.

On the way back to the priest's house, my dad told me that Josie and my cousin, Margaret, had gone to Fort Smith for training at the hospital. They would come home for the summer months. He also told me that he was now living with my Uncle Louie and his family. We stopped at the Bay store and bought a few things we needed for our trip back home.

We spent the night at the priest's residence. The next morning, my dad thanked the priest and we packed up our belongings. We walked to West Channel on a trail along the shore. It was a long walk, and when we finally arrived, we put our bags and other things into the canoe. Then we sat on a log and waited for the two men who were to take us back to Fort Providence. While we waited, my dad asked about my trip and what I had seen down south. I told him about some of my experiences on the farm, and about seeing new things like drive-in movies, drive-in restaurants, and so on.

I mentioned seeing the people in Meander River who spoke Slavey. He told me that the Dene people lived all over the place. There were Dene people who lived near High Level. Some of the Dene people in Hay River came from these places.

Finally, the men arrived with their belongings and a couple of cases of beer. Apparently, they had been drinking uptown while we waited for them. We loaded the canoe and pushed off to prepare to leave. The two men sat in the back of the canoe and one of them started the kicker. We made our way out onto the lake and headed north on our way to Big Island. The men drank beer once in awhile as we travelled along the south shore of the lake.

My dad looked concerned for our safety, but he didn't say anything. We travelled through the night and I slept off and on like I had done on the bus. I'd wake up whenever the men stopped the kicker to fill the gas tank.

In the early morning light, as we got closer to Fort Providence, I began to recognize some of the familiar places along the shore. I recognized Dory Point as we went by. From there, travelling would be faster with the swift current. As we rounded the point by the present-day Big River service station, we could see the familar grey building and the big church.

Soon, we arrived in the settlement, and once we landed, my dad picked up our bags and we walked up the steep riverbank. Once we reached the top, we rested awhile. In the distance, I saw a few tents in the field behind the Hudson's Bay compound. We picked up our things and I followed my dad to my uncle's house. My Uncle Louie and his wife were both up and about. I shook hands with them and my aunt offered us something to eat.

While we ate, my uncle made small-talk with my dad. He

mentioned something about mending the nets in preparation for the fall fishing season. After eating, my dad said he would like to rest for awhile and I followed him to our tent behind the house. It had been a long trip for me to get back home and the rest would be welcome. I followed my dad into the tent, lay down on the bedding, closed my eyes and went to sleep.

CHAPTER SIXTEEN

After I came back from my trip south, I stayed with my dad for about four or five days before it was time for all of us to go back to the residential school. I went with my dad to see Father Superior to ask if I could stay with him for a while longer, as I hadn't seen him all summer. To my surprise, the Father gave his permission, but it was on the condition that I went to school every day and made sure I attended mass on Sundays. Naturally, I readily agreed.

During this time, I went hunting for ducks and geese with my dad and uncle as often as I could. We spent one weekend around the Big Island area at the mouth of the Mackenzie River, camping on Birch Island on the North Channel. It was sure nice to be out on the land, cooking out, smelling the fire and sleeping under the stars. It reminded me a lot of my childhood days. I stayed with my dad and uncle until they were ready to leave for their fall fishing camp.

Once I was back in the residential school again, I felt a little homesick, like I usually did, wishing I could be with my dad. I went to school but I was a little restless, remembering some of the things I had seen and done down south that summer. I thought about the idea of going to school there, but this seemed like a very remote possibility.

Going to school didn't seem like a big challenge to me anymore, especially in Fort Providence. I was there mainly because I was required by law to be at the residential school until I was of age to be on my own. I felt I needed to go somewhere else, to learn something new and different. Maybe I could go to some other school to learn to be a teacher and teach in another community. All this was going on in my mind and I really didn't know what to do.

Finally one day, I got up enough nerve to see Father Superior. I asked if he could send me down south to go to school. I thought that because I was now thirteen years old, the Father might consider it. He chuckled, yet he was also surprised at my request. Then he asked me why I wanted the transfer. Was I not happy being taught and looked after by the Sisters? I assured him that I was happy, but told him maybe I would be able to learn more and be able to see other places if I went away to another school.

Then he said there was a nice Catholic school down south that was run by some religious Brothers; maybe I could go there. I looked at the floor and just shrugged my shoulders. After all this time at the residential school, I was good at doing that – looking at the floor and shrugging my shoulders whenever I stood in front of the priest or Sister to explain some perceived wrongdoing that I was usually not aware of.

I asked again if he thought I could go to school down south. He told me the Bishop was due for his last summer visit to Fort Providence soon, and he would talk to him. He seemed a little confused as to how he should respond to my request. Maybe it was a good thing the Bishop was coming for a visit.

I left the Fathers' residence feeling elated and hopeful the Bishop would grant his permission. I thought about the possibility of going to school in Edmonton and perhaps living with Ron's brother-in-law and his family. After all, I knew them and they were my friends. Then I remembered that long bus ride and immediately thought about the possibility of flying to Edmonton, instead. Little did I know then that this was all a big dream, but once again, I waited in anticipation for the Bishop's plane to arrive. The days seemed to drag on and on.

My dad came to visit when he and my uncle came to town with a load of fish. I didn't say anything to him about my request to Father Superior about going to school down south. I thought I would tell him just before the visit was over. My dad asked if I wanted to buy some candies at the mission store. I told him I had to get permission from the Sister, which I did. Then we walked over and Father Superior opened the little store for us.

While we were in the store, Father Superior told my dad about my request to go to school down south. Then he asked my dad what he thought about that. My dad replied that I was now in the care of the Sisters and it would seem that it was their responsibility to make that decision. He went on to say that he would go along with whatever decision was made as long as I came home for the summer to be with him. The Father told my dad that he was sure that I would be allowed to come home for the summer months. Then he asked my dad to come by the next time he was in town. By then, he'd know for sure if I was still there or had gone with the Bishop.

After our visit was over, my dad left the building and I returned to the boys' section. It was then that I thought if I went away down south, I wouldn't be able to see my dad until school was over in the summer. There wouldn't be any home visits at Christmas or Easter. What if I wasn't able to go home, like some of the boys at the residential school? Then it would be a long time before I saw my dad again. But I really wanted to go to school down south, so I tried to think of something else a little more pleasant.

⤵

A few days later, while we were playing outside, we heard the sound of a distant plane. The Bishop's plane had finally arrived!

As usual, the Bishop stayed for the next couple of days. Meanwhile, I waited in anticipation for some word about my request. I didn't know for sure if I would be going anywhere, as there had been no indication from anyone that my request was either being granted or denied, or even talked about. Still, I hoped and waited.

Then on the third day of the Bishop's visit, the Sister called me into the building. I was nervous, as I knew what it was all about. I hoped it was good news. As I came into the recreation area, she told me that I would be leaving with the Bishop. I stopped and tried not to show too much emotion, so I just nodded my head. Two other boys were in the room; they would also be going along. Then the Sister asked us to collect our stuff and pack our clean clothes for the trip.

For the rest of the day, I thought about nothing but leaving and going down south. I would finally be leaving the residential school! After lunch, we took our suitcases down to the docking area. Soon the Bishop arrived, followed by the priests, Brothers and some Sisters, and the boys and girls from the residential school. As usual, he made his rounds among the assembled people on the riverbank, eventually making his way down to the shore. The pilot helped him walk up the plank from the shore to the pontoon and into the plane where we waited. The plane taxied out onto the river and took off, with the pilot making his customary circle over the settlement before flying off into the direction of Hay River.

I was finally leaving Fort Providence and the residential school. By this time, I had spent seven years at the Sacred Heart Residential School. During that time, I was able to go home every summer for two months. So out of the seven years, I had spent a total of one year and two months at home. I went through the system, despite the many personal hardships. I learned how to deal with it by trial and error. Eventually, I just did what the Sister told me without question, just to stay out of trouble, and learned to quietly and patiently suffer through the ordeal without emotion, hoping it would end one day. For lack of a better word, I guess I can say I persevered.

After a short flight along the Mackenzie River and across the southern part of the Great Slave Lake, we landed in Hay River. A priest was waiting on the dock. He was the same priest I had met when I returned from Edmonton on the bus. The Brother threw him a rope and he tied up the pontoon to the dock. As we got off the plane, the Bishop told us to wait by the dock, then the priest led the Bishop and pilot down the trail towards town.

One of the boys said we were probably going to Fort Smith, where the Bishop lived in a big house. I wondered then if we were going to take the plane from Fort Smith to Edmonton, which started me thinking again about staying with Ron's brother-in-law and his family. I wondered how far the school was from their house, and whether I was going to walk or take the bus to school. All these things were going through my mind as we waited for the Bishop. I had great expectations.

We sat around on the dock and waited for what seemed like a very long time. Finally, we heard them talking as they came walking out of the bush on the trail. Once we were all back in the plane, the Bishop asked if any of us had ever been to Fort Resolution. He said it was a nice place and that he had to go there for a short visit. I thought to myself, the short visit would probably end up being the usual two or three days.

The plane taxied up the river and slowly turned around before taking off over the Great Slave Lake. After a few more minutes, the plane turned inland and followed the shoreline to Fort Resolution. Soon, we were flying over the settlement. From the air, I could see a large dock on the lakeshore that was shaped like a big number seven. The plane circled over the town and gently landed on the water.

As the plane approached the dock, the Bishop turned to us and said, "Well, boys, here we are. I hope you will like your new home." I looked up and thought— what! Was this as far south as I would go? Where would I go to school? Whatever happened to Edmonton? Was this what I had been waiting anxiously for all these days? This was sure a big surprise! True, Fort Resolution was south of Fort Providence across the Great Slave Lake; at least I was headed in the right direction, although I ended up at the wrong place.

We waited as the Bishop made his way out of the plane and chatted to a priest on the shore. Then we all got off and waited again as the Brother took our bags out of the plane. There were many people milling around on the dock, and the

Bishop was walking among them and shaking hands.

The trip wasn't what I had expected but there was one consolation: I met Ron and Walter again. It was nice to see familiar faces among the strangers. We picked up our bags and followed Ron and Walter up the path past the Hudson's Bay store. They were supervising at the senior boys' residence, which was known locally as the Brown House.

The building had been renovated with sleeping quarters upstairs in a large, attic-type room with a low ceiling. There were a couple rows of beds, and a couple of bunks against the wall. There were about ten or twelve of us in a group at the Brown House.

I no longer had Sisters supervising or teaching me now. Those of us who stayed at the Brown House went to classes at the residential school, but at least here, I was able to live with the senior boys away from the residential school.

⁂

It was fall and the weather was getting colder. Each day, more ice formed along the shores of the Great Slave Lake. The lake froze evenly for a hundred yards or so from the shore. Beyond that, the ice was piled up in jagged pieces after it was broken up by the waves. There was still open water further out on the lake.

We went skating along the lakeshore. Most of the boys and girls from the residential school were also out skating or walking around on the ice. It was great because the shore seemed endless and we could skate forever. It was possible to skate right up to Hay River, but it would probably take the better part of a day.

The weather continued to get colder every day; it snowed

off and on, until one day, the snow came to stay. It covered the field by the old hospital, making the field appear larger than it actually was. The snow also covered the cords of firewood stacked by the barn.

One day, a couple of the Brothers and some of the boys started putting up some boards close to the barn in the girls' section of the yard. I was told it would be for a skating rink. This was going to be a regular-sized skating rink, a far cry from our little rink in For Providence with its single planks for walls.

Before supper that evening, the Brothers began flooding the rink. A fine, foggy mist rose into the air as the water flowed over the frozen ground. The water came from a long hose that ran from the building. The boys didn't have to haul pails of water to flood the rink like we did back home.

The next evening, our supervisor said that we could use the rink after supper. We would be the first ones to go skating on the newly flooded rink, which was lit up with light bulbs hanging from a single electrical line running above its entire length.

Some of the boys brought along their hockey sticks and knocked a puck around against the boards. These boys had actual hockey sticks, not like the homemade ones we had back home at the residential school. One of the boys even let me use his hockey stick for awhile.

Later, the boys put their hockey sticks aside and we started playing tag. This was not like your regular tag game. Our supervisors, Ron and Walter, had taught us this tag game back in Fort Providence. One boy would be "it" and he stood at centre ice. The rest of us lined up at one end of the rink.

Once the "it" boy counted up to three we'd all skate towards him as fast as we could to avoid being tagged. Once someone was tagged, he would go to the side of the rink. Sometimes we'd play free-for-all tag. This was a little more fun, as once someone was tagged, he could help the "it" boy to tag the rest of the players. In the free-for-all tag, the faster skaters were usually the last ones to be tagged. This was a lot of fun, but it was also very tiring, especially on our first day of skating.

There were also organized hockey games between actual teams. Some of the players, especially the Public School teachers, actually had uniforms, complete with shoulder pads and shin pads. We wore pieces of cardboard under our jeans for our shin pads. We didn't have hockey gloves; we just used our regular gloves or mitts. It was my first time watching an organized hockey game. It was also my first time playing in an organized hockey game, and it was a lot of fun.

The Brown House was located in the boys' yard, some distance from the skating rink. I remember one time, one of the older boys had written a note to one of the senior girls. I was one of the few younger boys who lived at the Brown House, so I was asked by this older boy to deliver the note. He said someone would be waiting, so I walked to the girls' section of the yard and delivered the note to the girl who was waiting at the bottom of the stairs leading up to the senior girls' dorm. This was easy.

Another time on one of these delivery trips, I put on my skates and walked to the rink carrying a puck and my hockey stick. When I got to the rink, I turned on the lights. Almost immediately, one of the girls came running down the stairs. I walked over and she asked for the note. I didn't even know if it was meant for her, but she took the note and asked me to wait. I walked back to the rink and skated around, knocking the puck against the boards and listening as it echoed into the night.

After awhile, the girl came down the stairs and called me over. This time, she handed me a note. It must have been a reply to the note I had brought earlier. I went back to the rink and turned off the lights, then made my way back to the Brown House with the note safely tucked into my shirt pocket. For my troubles, I would usually get some candies, or sometimes a cigarette.

I often wondered what was written in some of those notes. Had I read some of them, I certainly would have had a totally different story to tell on this page. But having been raised in the residential school, there were a few things you learned not to do to avoid trouble, or to avoid committing a sin. So the notes were delivered unread. Mind you, the temptation was there.

∽

It was around the beginning of December when our supervisors told us we would all be leaving Fort Resolution. We were moving to Fort Smith to a brand new hostel and school, and they would also be moving with us. Now, this move was a little further south than Fort Resolution and a little closer to Edmonton. Going away to school in the south was still on my mind.

Some of us were pretty excited about moving to another new town. A few boys were from Fort Smith, but most of us had never been there. During the week between Christmas and New Year's, all the boys and girls from the residential school began leaving for Fort Smith. Some of the supervising

Sisters also left with them. Over the next few days, the schoolyard was strangely quiet when we went for our meals at the residential school. Then a day or two before the New Year, a big plane arrived to take the rest of us to Fort Smith. I think the big plane was the Wardair's Bristol, possibly the same one which now sits as a monument by the Yellowknife Airport.

The front end of the plane opened up and a ramp came down to the ground. We went up the ramp in single file with our suitcases and bags. Some of us sat along the wall and faced each other, while a few of the boys sat at the back on a row of seats. We felt the plane move as it taxied out on the runway to take off. It shook as its engines roared loudly and lifted in the air on our way to Fort Smith. It was going to be about a one-hour trip. Occasionally, the plane shook and bounced up and down a little while some of us tried to nap. At last, we felt the big plane banking as it approached the airport. It landed with a slight bump, and we were in Fort Smith.

Once we were all out of the plane, we were met by our supervisors. They walked us through the airport building and out into a waiting school bus. We were driven to the new hostel, Breynat Hall, which was located behind the new J.B.Tyrell School. This began my experience with the hostel system. From then on, I would no longer have religious supervisors, just regular, lay people.

We settled into our new surroundings in no time. I was glad to be there, because Josie and Margaret were in town training and working at the local hospital. I didn't know where the hospital was located or how to get in touch with them, but I was sure my sister would come and visit me when she found out I was at the new hostel.

Josie did come for many visits, sometimes with Margaret. I would go uptown to the stores with them, especially on weekends, and sometimes I would see them at the local baseball games. The following year, Josie and Margaret completed their training and went home.

For the remaining school year in Fort Smith, I went to J. B. Tyrell School to finish grade eight. Then the following year, I went to the Public School uptown for grade nine. There, I was the only Dene among the other white and Métis grade nine students. I didn't mind, though, because no one said anything strange to me and I was treated like everyone else.

Among the school subjects, grade nine French was the easiest for me as I had learned French during my early days at the residential school. It was probably one of the few good things that came out of there for me. My math and history teacher was quite a person. He'd ask questions on math or history, then walk around waiting for an answer from anyone. He'd look around at us with red veins showing on his face and neck, like he expected one of us to jump up and give him a correct answer immediately. This was the impression he gave, at least to me.

One day, he asked me a question on some math equation. I gave him the wrong answer, and he said, "That's not it, idiot." I could have crawled under my desk; I was so embarrassed. I was sitting close to the front of the class and I could feel some of my classmates looking at me. Maybe they weren't, but it felt like all eyes were on me at that instant. Another time during history class, we were reading about Jean de Brebeuf and his Jesuit companions who were burned at the stake by the Huron or Iroquois Indians. The same teacher asked the class, "Why do you think the Indians did that?"

There was silence; then he came over to my desk and asked me directly the same question. He seemed to imply that being an Indian, I should know the answer. However, I didn't say anything because I had no answer to his question. Then he moved on to another student's desk for the answer.

Thereafter, I felt really self-conscious, not only in history class but also in other classes. I stayed quiet most times and wouldn't answer any questions in class. I only answered a question if and when I knew for sure that I had the right answer, and I continued to do this right to the end of my high school years.

⌒

I received some news from home during the spring of my second year in Fort Smith: my sister was getting married. She was marrying a man named Fred. I knew Fred's family and his two younger brothers were around my age. Apparently, she had written a letter to tell me all about it, but her letter had arrived after the wedding date. I doubted very much that the Father would have allowed me to go home for an event such as a wedding. At least I would get to see my sister again in the summer.

At the end of the school year, I wrote my grade nine departmental exams and went home for the summer like the rest of the other kids.

There was usually not very much going on work-wise in Fort Providence, but that summer, Canadian National Telegraph (CNT) was running a telephone line from Hay River to Yellowknife. About two weeks after coming home from Fort Smith, I got a summer job with CNT with some of the men from Fort Providence. I thought the job would last all summer but it only lasted about three weeks.

We worked on Meridian Island for awhile, until the line was ready to be strung underwater across the river to Fort Providence. The idea was to bury the cable under the water from Meridian Island to Green Island, which was located in the middle of the Mackenzie River right across from the settlement. From there, the cable would run over the western tip of the island and back underwater to the mainland on the north side of the river. The cable would come up onto the shore by the present-day Nursing Station. There were a couple of huge telephone poles already in place at that site.

We did all that work just to keep the cable underwater. However, the following spring, I heard the ice had dug up the cable during the break-up, so it had to be cut. When I went home for a couple of days the following summer, I saw the cable. This time, it was strung across the river, high above the water.

It was sometime during the summer when the local RCMP officer informed me that I had passed the grade nine departmental exams. I would be going to Yellowknife for high school in the fall. But at that time, I wasn't quite sure if I really wanted to go back to school. I was still working at my summer job and I didn't want to quit. I thought maybe I could work until the job was finished, when the line reached Yellowknife.

Over the next few days, I thought about it. Finally, I mentioned to my dad that I considered not going back to school in the fall. He asked if I had thought of what I was going to do, and I told him that I could work until my summer job was completed. He then asked what I was going to do after that. I replied that I could come back home after the job was done and go trapping for the winter. My dad then asked if I had traps and equipment like a toboggan, harness and a dog team. He continued, noting I would also probably need a tent, stove, stove pipes, an axe and blankets. I told him that maybe I could go with someone who had all the equipment for trapping, to which he said that going with someone who had all the trapping equipment did not mean he would lend me any traps. I thought, why is he making this so difficult? All I wanted to do was work until my job was over, and then go trapping like some of my friends from the residential school had done.

Then one day at work, the foreman came over and told us the workers from Fort Providence would be laid off. They didn't need labourers anymore and their crew was moving camp up the highway. Now that my summer job was over, this brought a whole new perspective to my situation. A few days later, I told my dad that I had been laid off from work. He said I could go back to school or go trapping; it was my choice.

I often wondered about this episode with my dad. In his own way, he let me know what it took to be a good trapper. At that time, there was really nothing much for me to do in Fort Providence, and he probably knew that, too. The only available choice for me was to go trapping, and I didn't have the necessary equipment. I sometimes wonder what I would be doing today if I had stayed home and gone trapping. My life experiences would surely have been very different.

My Friends (left to right): Andy Mandeville, Edward McLeod and me

CHAPTER SEVENTEEN

After that brief discussion with my dad about trapping, I decided to go back to school, at least for grade ten. I left Fort Providence in late August on the bus and headed for Yellowknife, and to a high school in another new place. At that time in Yellowknife, there was a new hostel called Akaitcho Hall and a new school: Sir John Franklin.

Hostel life at Akaitcho Hall was certainly a new experience for me. Instead of the large dormitories that I was accustomed to, we were assigned four to a room. There were two sets of bunks, closets and dressers, and desks by the window for doing homework. There, I lived and went to school with Inuit, Métis, white and even Chinese students. This was quite a change for me from the residential school days. Living at the hostel at that time proved to be a good experience for me in later life. It taught me to get along with and respect people from other cultures, to treat them like you would anyone else.

The hostel was located on a rocky hill overlooking part of the Yellowknife Bay and the Great Slave Lake. The school building was located just below the hostel, so I didn't have too far to walk, especially on cold winter mornings. There was even a set of stairs from the side door of the hostel that led to a landing close to the school door.

The day after I arrived at the hostel, I went to the school with some of the other students for registration and enrolled in grade ten studies. When classes began, I would go to my home-room for the first lesson of the day. Then I would go to different classrooms for other subjects taught by different teachers. This was another new experience for me. Previously, I would stay in the same classroom all day.

Sir John Franklin was a composite high school, so there were all kinds of activities going on. Besides academic studies, there were courses offered in mechanics, carpentry, heavy equipment and home economics.

Sitting by the window in the classroom one day, I saw one of my friends operating a grader. He was clearing and pushing the freshly fallen snow to the far end of the schoolyard. Another student was operating a loader, picking up the snow and dropping it into the back of a dump truck. I thought to myself, I wouldn't mind learning how to operate some of that heavy equipment. It would give me a chance to get outdoors and maybe get a job on the highway someday.

The next afternoon, I went to see the school principal. I wasn't nervous or scared; this wasn't like asking Father Superior to send me to school down south. I just wanted to change my study program. I asked him if I could drop my academic studies because I wanted to take up training as a heavy equipment operator.

The principal listened politely to my request, then said, "Why don't you continue with your grade ten studies for the next couple of weeks? After that, if you still want to be a heavy equipment operator, we'll see what can be done."

I wasn't disappointed, because he hadn't told me I couldn't switch programs. I would just stay where I was for the time being. Now, I had a couple of weeks to think about dropping my grade ten studies and learning to be a heavy equipment operator, or just finishing my academic program.

⌘

Life at Akaitcho Hall was completely different from what I was used to. At the residential school, we had the Grey Nuns supervising us. That was still the case in some hostels like Fort Simpson and Fort Smith. But here in Yellowknife, the boys were supervised by men and the girls were supervised by women. We had freedom, based on an individual honour system. This was a great improvement from the residential school system.

We did have chores to do, like washing dishes, sweeping floors and hallways, and doing general clean-up on Saturdays. We were allowed to go uptown after school, and we were even given weekly allowances to go to movies. Our student cards enabled us to get in for fifty cents or one dollar. If we didn't go to the movies, we went to watch the local hockey action at the Gerry Murphy Arena. We also had dances on Friday and Saturday evenings in the cafeteria/recreation area. Music was provided through a record player connected to a loud speaker.

At Akaitcho Hall, a few of the boys had guitars and there were other instruments in the common room. Sometimes, a few of the boys would get together and play to pass the time. John, the boys' supervisor, noticed this was going on and took an interest, encouraging us to play and sing.

At first we got together just for fun. But eventually, with out supervisor's help, we formed a band. There were five or six of us, and we called ourselves the Arctic Ramblers. We had guitars, fiddle, bass guitar, drums, and there was even a piano for awhile. We practiced whenever we could.

Eventually, we had a chance to play at a dance in the dining area at Akaitcho Hall. After that, when we were all available, we would sometimes play at weekend dances at Akaitcho Hall. We even had the opportunity to travel to Hay River to play for a school dance. We travelled in a couple of vehicles, crossing the Mackenzie River in early April when it was frozen over.

On the return trip, however, water was beginning to pool along the shore. We all got out and walked across the river on top of the still-frozen snow banks, as the supervisors drove the vehicles back across. We really didn't think it was dangerous; we saw it as an adventure.

When I first saw The Chieftones practice at the St. Albert Residential School gym, it reminded me a lot of my first band experience at Akaitcho Hall. I realized back then that I could sing and play in front of an audience, but it never occurred to me that one day I would make it a brief career.

Time went by, and we were getting ready to go home for Christmas holidays. By that time, I had completely forgotten about being a heavy equipment operator. The principal never did call me into his office again, nor did he ever mention the matter to me. Years later, I was thankful for what he had done, and for what he hadn't done. What he did was to let things carry on as usual; and what he didn't do was to grant my request to train as a heavy equipment operator. I went on to finish grade ten that year.

✐

That spring of my first year in Yellowknife, we all attended the graduation ceremonies for the grade twelve students. The principal was handing out awards to some of the students. I never expected anything, so I was surprised when he called out my name. I had won an award for literature, although I wasn't aware that I was proficient at it. Actually, literature was really not one of my better school subjects. We had read some Shakespeare and other books, but when it came to writing essays, I had a terrible time trying to find anything to write about. Some of the other students in my class didn't have that problem.

One time I wrote about the game of hockey. It was something that I knew and could write about. Perhaps I could have written about my early experiences living on the land with my parents, or about some other experiences at the residential school, but at that time, it didn't seem relevant to what I was being taught in school. I thought my teachers and classmates wouldn't be interested in that. I suppose at that time in my teenage life, I had a limited point of view.

Nevertheless, I had been selected to attend the Shake-spearean Festival in Stratford, Ontario with other students from across Canada, and I was happy to accept the award. It was going to be another new experience for me. I was to leave about the middle of July. Meanwhile, school was over and I took a summer job with a small local painting firm. The boss was a likeable fellow named Bill, who also became a friend. Over the years, I'd run into him now and then when I was in Yellowknife and we'd chat for awhile. I explained to him that I had the chance to attend a festival with other students from across Canada. I would have to leave for a couple of weeks, if that was all right with him, but I wanted to work for him again when I returned. Bill agreed, and told me it would be a good opportunity for me to see another part of the country.

Soon the day came for me to leave for Stratford. I flew to Edmonton, where I was met by a teacher from Whitehorse. She would be the chaperone on this trip for the Northwest Territories and Yukon students. The next day, we boarded a train that would take us to Toronto. Once the train was underway, we were allowed to walk around and meet some of the other students. The train travelled on, and there were many stops to pick up more students. The porter told us there was an observation car up ahead, so a few of us made our way forward. The car had an upper deck with a glass dome roof, and one could see off into the distance as the train sped on.

It was late into the night when we crossed the prairies on our way to Regina. We sat in the observation car and watched the lights scattered here and there. Some were far off in the distance, which made it seem like we were crossing a lake at night. When we returned to our coach, the porter made up our beds and bunks from our seats. In the morning, we took turns having breakfast in the dining car.

The train continued on, stopping for more students, and travelling on by Lake Superior, Armstrong and Sudbury. The next stop would be Toronto. I think the entire train trip took two days.

At the Toronto train station, we all got off and made our way out to some buses that were waiting for us. We travelled through the city and out into the country on our way to Stratford, where we were all assigned billets. The next day, we toured the Stratford theatre, saw the dressing rooms of the actors, and watched the ending of a rehearsal. We even went under the stage and some of us came up through the trapdoors on the stage floor. The guide also showed us a small speaker in one of the pillars onstage. If an actor forgot his lines, he would stroll nonchalantly over to the pillar, and the director or stagehand would whisper the words, and the play would carry on.

During the next few days at the Stratford festival I saw my first stage plays. Among the Shakespearean plays I saw was *A Midsummer Night's Dream,* with a young Bruno Gerussi playing the part of Puck. I think he was also in the play *Romeo and Juliet.* Another young actor, who could have been Christopher Plummer, appeared in *King Lear.* I also saw my very first and only opera: *H.M.S. Pinafore.*

The return trip to Yellowknife was enjoyable; maybe it was because by then, most of us knew each other. Some of the students had guitars and we would have sing-a-longs. It was sad to say goodbye as some students got off, and there were a few tears during such moments. We made many friends on that trip, and some of us wrote to each other once we got back to our home communities. When I arrived in Yellowknife, I went back to my summer job until the last week in August.

⌒

By the end of August, students began arriving at Akaitcho Hall. Some were returning and others were new arrivals. The first couple of days into September, we all registered for classes and I began my grade eleven studies.

During this time, I took up some sports I had never played before. I started playing badminton, basketball and volleyball at the school gym in the evenings. We even had an evening of free skating at the Gerry Murphy Arena for the Akaitcho

Hall students. I joined up for a hockey team—The Seals. Our coach was a member of the local RCMP detachment.

There was one player on our team who had never skated before in his life. But he persevered, and soon he was able to move around. By that, I mean he was just able to move around. When he was on the ice and the puck came to him, he would swing at it with his hockey stick. Most times, he would miss, and the momentum would spin him around. He'd spin around for a few moments and then he'd fall. He also leaned heavily on his hockey stick, so when he lifted the stick to hit the puck, he'd lose his balance. The players from the other team used to lift his hockey stick, just for the fun of it. It was funny to see, but we all had a great time.

∽

While still in high school, I got a part-time job with the local CBC radio—CFYK. The radio station was located in the basement of what was the old Tree of Peace Friendship Centre building. I did some local news and public service announcements in South Slavey, and played some records, mostly country music.

Eventually, we started doing a request program that became known as "Gather Round". The listeners would send in their requests, and if we had the record we'd play it on the air. The program was broadcast on Saturday afternoons.

Initially, I would go to the studio and record the program on Friday evenings for the Saturday afternoons show. Then eventually, we did some live broadcasts. During the live broadcasts I would sit or stand in a small booth, about the size of a telephone booth. One of the other announcers would operate the equipment for me and I would read the request letters. Some of the request letters we received were fairly long, and there were times when we received quite a lot of mail for the program. Gather Round went on to be a popular program on CBC radio. It ran for many seasons in different time slots, but usually in the same format. After being away for a few years, I returned to Yellowknife and got back on with CBC. Gather Round was still around!

❧

During my second year at Akaitcho Hall, a National Film Board crew came to Yellowknife from Montreal to do a documentary on Akaitcho Hall and Sir John Franklin School. The film crew went around filming short takes here and there before they filmed some larger scenes with the students. The story centred around one of the Inuit boys from the Delta. The film crew followed him around, taking short shots that were rehearsed and some that were not rehearsed. They filmed dances and other recreational activities. I was also in the film, as the crew came to CBC one day to film me working at the console.

Before the school year was out, we saw the completed film. I think it was entitled *Arctic Campus*. We all had a few laughs at some of the scenes, but it wasn't bad as a short documentary on life at the school and hostel. It was the only time I ever saw that film. Some years later, when I was working at the National Film Board in Montreal, I went through their catalogue of existing films looking for that documentary but I never did find *Arctic Campus* on the list. The National Film Board had taken it off their circulation list, so it's probably sitting on a shelf somewhere collecting dust.

When school was over, I got a summer job with the federal Department of Public Works. We surveyed a cut line that later turned out to be part of the Simpson Highway. Four of us from Akaitcho Hall were hired as part of the survey crew. We flew to Hay River and were met by another worker who took us to the camp, which was located about five miles in the bush off the highway at the present-day Simpson Highway junction. The driver followed the cut lines and parts of the old winter road. It took us about an hour and a half to get to the camp, as there were times when we had to winch the truck out of the soft ground.

After a tiring journey, we finally arrived at the camp. There were three trailers set up on the banks of a small lake; two were used for the crew's sleeping quarters and the third was for the cook house and dining area. A small shed with a generator supplied power to the camp.

After about three weeks on the job, we were given a weekend off. We went to Fort Providence because it was only about twenty miles away. On the ferry, we met a taxi driver returning to Yellowknife. We bought about two or three bottles of liquor from him. This was my first time buying a bootlegged bottle. The ferry landed, and we drove off and went into town. We visited a friend of mine who had a tent behind his parent's house. There, we proceeded with an all-night party.

Sometime in the early morning hours, I began to throw up. I was feeling pretty drunk, and was no longer in a party mood, so I made my way over to my uncle's house where my dad was staying. I knocked on the door and my dad opened it. He looked surprised to see me and asked if I had been drinking. I told him I had been drinking with some friends. Then he said he hoped my friends had a place for me to sleep, and closed the door in my face. I think my dad was angry because I hadn't gone to see him like I usually did when I came into town. He was probably also upset to see me drunk.

I walked behind the house and sat on the grass by the back wall. Then I put my head in my hands and cried, feeling really sorry for my drunken self. Next to the shed behind the house was a tent, and I crawled inside. I lay down a tarp and fell asleep, oblivious to the mosquitoes buzzing around me. A few hours later, sometime past noon, I woke up to the sound of people talking. It was hot in the tent and I was sweating. I got up and walked to the outside fireplace. My aunt and uncle were there, having something to eat. My uncle offered me some food but I declined. I told him I had a very bad headache and I didn't feel like eating. Then in Slavey he said something like, "I guess that's what happens when people drink."

I was eighteen years old and suffering through my first hangover. It was an awful mixture of feelings. I kept thinking, why did I buy that bottle and drink? I just wanted to lie down for a few more hours and sleep it off. Maybe I would wake up feeling much better.

After that episode, for the next few years, I never got that drunk again. Oh, I drank all right, but only a beer or two. I became more of a social drinker when I worked and travelled in the States. It wasn't until I was twenty-five years old and back home that I began some serious drinking. Then it was party time most weekends. But I'm happy to say now that I have been sober for many years.

Once I left Fort Providence to complete my grade nine in Fort Smith, I never really went back to live. I came home only for a day or two and I was gone again. When school was over, I usually got summer jobs that took me away. Most of the time, I returned directly back to school in Yellowknife from the job site. There were times when Josie had to track me down to get a message to me from my dad or someone else.

After I left Akaitcho Hall and Sir John Franklin High School, I got a job at Con Mine as a replacement for another worker who was going on an extended three-month holiday. At the job site, I was introduced to a man named Nolan who was to train me on the job as a sampler. For the first few days, I went underground with Nolan and collected rock samples. Then he showed me how to grade the rocks and update the map. The map was of the underground levels where I was to go to pick up samples.

From Con Mine I went to another job in Norman Wells. Everything went well during that summer, until one Saturday morning when one of the boys called in sick and I took his shift. That morning, I had an accident and lost part of my index finger. I was taken to the company hospital, where the doctor bandaged up my hand.

I stayed in the company hospital for about four days after my accident. Then I went to the University Hospital in Edmonton, accompanied by the company doctor. There, I was examined and given six weeks off work for rehabilitative therapy. At the end of this, the doctor gave my hand a final examination and I returned to Yellowknife.

Shortly thereafter, I went to Fort Smith to work at the Indian Affairs Regional Office as a trainee. The work was mostly doing general office procedures: making files and filing, sometimes typing letters, updating Band lists, and so on. I worked in Fort Smith all winter and into the following spring.

I was beginning to enjoy the work and thought possibly of staying in Fort Smith for some time. Then suddenly, at the end of May, I found out that my training was over. So in June, I packed my belongings and returned home to Fort Providence for a few days. At least I'd be home for my birthday.

By this time of year, all the ice was gone except for the odd, large pieces that came from the big lake and continued floating downriver until they melted away. During this brief time, I got a chance to go out on the land. It was spring, and there were many ducks and geese flying in from the south. I was out with my brother-in-law's two brothers and my dad, heading by canoe up to the mouth of the Mackenzie River and around the Big Island and Birch Island areas. We shot a few ducks and geese, and caught some fish. The fresh game and fish sure tasted good cooked over the open fire. It was refreshing just to be back out on the land.

During this time, I wasn't really sure of what I wanted to do career-wise. I had completed grade twelve and now I could go to college or look for a job for the winter. The prospects of finding a winter job didn't look too good, so I thought maybe I should try college. I had been thinking of this off and on, but now time was running out and I had to make up my mind.

One day I made up my mind and got on a bus and went south to Edmonton. I had planned to get into one of the study programs at Alberta College for the fall semester, and I would to stay with my cousin, Leon, until I found my own place. He was supervising at the residential school in St. Albert. As I sat on the bus, I wondered where I would have been and what I would have been doing if the principal at Sir John Franklin High School had agreed to let me train as a heavy equipment operator.

I had the best intentions, but I never did go to college. At the St. Albert Residential School, I met four other Indian boys who had come from places in northern British Columbia like Terrace, Kitwanga, and Aiyansh. They had formed and were playing in a band they called The Chieftones. Some days, I watched them practice in the gym. Then one day, they invited me to sing a few songs with them, and eventually, I joined the band. Over the next few months, we played for dances and other events around the Edmonton area.

Then in November, we headed to Toronto and worked in the area for awhile. A few days before New Year's, we went south into the United States by way of Sault St. Marie, Michigan. We toured around the States for the next few years and met many other musicians. We even did a couple of recordings. We were booked through the William Morris Agency out of Chicago, and had a fan club based in Madison, Wisconsin. In New York City we appeared on national television, on a show called *To Tell the Truth*. The host of the show was Bud Collier, and we met a couple of the panel members: Orson Bean and a young Tom Poston, who later was on one of Bob Newhart's television sitcoms.

We did a brief tour across Canada, starting in London, Ontario, where we played at the Western Fair with a young Wayne Newton. Then we went west to the Lakehead Exhibition in Thunder Bay, on to the Regina Exhibition, the Klondike Days in Edmonton and ended up at the Pacific National Exhibition in Vancouver. After that, we went back into the States. The Chieftones even performed at President Nixon's inauguration ceremony in Washington. I missed out on this event, however, because I was back home at that time. Eventually, we became opening acts for some notable bands like the Beach Boys, Jerry Lee Lewis, and others.

At the hostel in Fort Smith, I used to listen to hockey games over the radio. Some of these took place at Madison Square Gardens and Boston Gardens. Now there I was, the boy from Lishamie, playing in a band in front of thousands of people, in the very same venues. It was something I never thought I would do, or ever dreamed could happen to me. My experience with The Chieftones took me far away from Lishamie, and it also took me temporarily away from the memories of the residential school.

CHAPTER EIGHTEEN

Drifting by Lishamie in a boat one spring day brought on a flood of memories. If only the old place could talk, I'm sure it would have many other stories to tell. The memories of my childhood were not only about the people and the old place, but mainly about my dad; he was, after all, the only parent I had known since I was seven years old. I knew I would lose him someday, but it is human nature to hang onto something we love and not think about ever losing them. Then one day, the inevitable happened and I was totally unprepared for it.

One day in September of 1972, I was living in Montreal and training at the National Film Board when I got a call that a family tragedy had happened. At that time, I was on a short assignment in Toronto, when I received word from the office that my dad had passed away.

Somehow Josie, with Margaret's help, tracked me down, just like she had tracked me down at various job sites over the years. She had even tracked me down in Boston a few years earlier, when my dad was very sick. I immediately checked out of the hotel and began the long drive back to Montreal. I tried not to think about anything; I just concentrated on driving and getting myself safely back to Montreal.

I was on a plane to Edmonton later that same evening. I stayed in Edmonton overnight, but I just couldn't sleep. I paced around in my room and went out for a short walk. I was tired the following morning when I flew to Yellowknife. My supervisor at NFB in Montreal had arranged a rented car for me, which I picked up at the Yellowknife airport and drove to Fort Providence.

It was more than a three-hour drive, so I had a lot of time to think about things. I remembered my dad talking about how things were before "the Sisters took you away," before my residential school days. He also mentioned how things were before "the white men took you away." This was in reference to my high school years and I think, in part, to my five years' absence while I lived and travelled in the States. I realized then that my dad, in his own way was trying to tell me something. I was to remember who I was and where I had come from at all times, now and in the future.

My dad and I spent time together like a father and son before my residential school days. But these became brief periods during the summer holidays, and our time together gradually came to an end after I left home to go to school and to summer job sites.

I had grown up in the residential school, away from my father's guidance. However, we did share a father and son relationship. He was a true, loving father to me, and I really hoped he hadn't regarded me as a son who grew up an arm's length away from him.

As I drove on, I thought of my mom, who had passed away so many years before, far from family and home. Then I remembered what she had said about my little brother passing away: "My poor little boy went away all alone among strangers." Now it was my dad who had passed away in Hay River, far from family and home.

I tried to remember some of the good times we had when I was growing up. Most of them happened when I was very young in Lishamie and during the summer months when I was home from the residential school. It was then that I began to remember some of the things that had happened to me in the residential school.

My personal experience at the residential school was not based entirely on physical, sexual and emotional abuse. Yes, there had been physical abuse, but more damaging was another form of abuse: the cultural and language loss as the result of my stay at the residential school. This situation affected other boys and girls my age, and other generations who experienced residential schools. The losses of language, spirituality, and traditional ways were the legacies of years of separation from our parents. Native children in the south experienced similar abuses and cultural losses long before we did in the Northwest Territories.

During my years at the residential school, I was deprived of family closeness in times of emotional and personal crisis. There was really no one I could talk to in times of need. The Sisters could not counsel me, so I was on my own to cope with a lot of life problems while growing up away from my parents.

The Sisters were only there to provide supervision and to ensure that we grew up to be good Catholics. They lacked compassion and child rearing skills, and appeared indifferent to the emotions of a child.

Sometimes I think the residential school was part of the government's efforts to impose cultural change upon the

Dene people. We were kept away from our parents and away from traditional activities intentionally, simply because they were considered obstacles to our progress into the so-called Christian and civilized society.

Today, we have words that adequately define and describe the residential school experience: forced assimilation, acculturation, fusion, and so on. The general public needs to understand that the impacts and effects of the residential school go far beyond the abuse of children that happened at the hands of the good-intentioned missionaries.

I began to think, if only I had been able to attend school from home, maybe things could have been different. I would have been able to spend more time with my dad. I arrived in Fort Providence and found Josie and her husband, Fred, and their two small children by the church. I got out of the car and she immediately ran over when she saw me. She hugged me and cried, thanking me for coming home. I assured her that I would have come no matter what. Then she told me that my dad had passed away due to some complications with pneumonia.

At my dad's funeral service the following day, my sister sobbed and wept until she almost lost her breath. The sound reminded me of my first day at the residential school, where I heard the desperate sobs from the newcomers. Strange that even at my dad's funeral, I had memories of the residential school. At a time when I should have been thinking of my dad and celebrating the good memories of his life, memories of the residential school crept into my mind.

Josie whispered that there was now only the two of us. I held her hand and told her there was her family; there was Archie, Daniel and their families. There were also many other cousins from Lishamie. She looked at me and said in our language, "You must have a strong heart because you don't cry easily." She continued crying while I held her hands. I decided then that I would stay on for a few extra days.

After the funeral service, I drove to the RCMP compound and asked to use the phone. I called the office in Montreal and got permission to stay over for a few more days. I spent all this time with my sister.

A couple of days after the funeral, I drove with Josie and her family for a picnic, out to a place we called the "Winter Crossing." Along the way she broke down and cried as she saw familiar places along the river, remembering times we had been there with our dad. Her children began to cry when they saw their mother crying. I found it difficult to deal with, but my brother-in-law comforted her.

A few days later, after many hugs and promises to write, I left Josie and her family for my return trip to Montreal. I had time to think about things again. As I was driving back to Yellowknife to catch the plane, I thought about my sister's words to me at my dad's funeral: *"You must have a strong heart because you don't cry easily."*

I realized then that I hadn't cried at all at the funeral, most likely because of the conditioning I had experienced at the residential school, where you learned to hide your emotions from the Sisters. I had tears in my eyes, but I never cried like my sister. I almost felt like an observer at my own dad's funeral. Maybe I really hadn't known my dad like I thought, because my childhood had been spent under the supervision of the Grey Nuns. I began to think of other things: what if I had done this, what if I had done that? If only things had happened differently. There suddenly seemed to be so many lost moments.

I remembered the summer months with my dad until I went away to Fort Smith. After that, I rarely came home for the summer. Maybe I had grown up an arm's length away from my dad. I drove to the side of the highway as tears began to fill my eyes.

I tried to remember the last time I saw my dad, and if there was anything important he might have said to me. He was probably lonely during the many years he was a widower, but I never thought to ask. He was always busy looking after us. I was glad I had an opportunity to have been with him, even if it was for a short while. Our time together was filled with happiness, and at times, with sadness, but I wouldn't change anything because it brought us closer together as a family.

Then suddenly, reality came in a rush as I realized that my dad was gone, the last remaining parent I had was really gone. I tried to remember my mom and the other members of my family who were also gone. There was now only me and my sister left of my original biological family.

I believed and hoped that my dad was now with my mom and my other brothers and sisters. He wouldn't hurt anymore; the pain was going to be my problem now, coping with life and all its pitfalls as a young man. I sat in the car on the side of the highway and cried like I should have cried with Josie at our dad's funeral.

And in that flood of emotion, I resolved to reconnect with Lishamie; it was my home, and my life began there, and perhaps, returning there would enable me to embark on my own personal healing journey.